FREE VIDEO FREE FREE VIDEO

Essential Test Tips Video from Trivium Test Prep

Dear Customer,

Thank you for purchasing from Trivium Test Prep! We're honored to help you prepare for your Praxis exam.

To show our appreciation, we're offering a **FREE *Praxis Essential Test Tips* Video by Trivium Test Prep**.* Our video includes 35 test preparation strategies that will make you successful on the Praxis. All we ask is that you email us your feedback and describe your experience with our product. Amazing, awful, or just so-so: we want to hear what you have to say!

To receive your **FREE *Praxis Essential Test Tips* Video**, please email us at 5star@ triviumtestprep.com. Include "Free 5 Star" in the subject line and the following information in your email:

1. The title of the product you purchased.
2. Your rating from 1 – 5 (with 5 being the best).
3. Your feedback about the product, including how our materials helped you meet your goals and ways in which we can improve our products.
4. Your full name and shipping address so we can send your **FREE *Praxis Essential Test Tips* Video**.

If you have any questions or concerns please feel free to contact us directly at 5star@triviumtestprep.com.

Thank you!

- Trivium Test Prep Team

*To get access to the free video please email us at 5star@triviumtestprep.com, and please follow the instructions above.

Praxis Core Study Guide 2021–2022

PRAXIS CORE ACADEMIC SKILLS FOR EDUCATORS
TEST PREP BOOK WITH READING, WRITING, AND
MATHEMATICS PRACTICE EXAM QUESTIONS
(5713, 5723, 5733)

Table of Contents

Online Resources

To help you fully prepare for your Praxis Core Academic Skills exam, Cirrus includes online resources with the purchase of this study guide.

PRACTICE TEST

In addition to the practice test included in this book, we also offer an online exam. Since many exams today are computer-based, getting to practice your test-taking skills on the computer is a great way to prepare.

FLASH CARDS

A convenient supplement to this study guide, Cirrus's e-flashcards enable you to review important terms easily on your computer or smartphone.

CHEAT SHEETS

Review the core skills you need to master with easy-to-read Cheat Sheets. Topics covered include Numbers and Operations, Algebra, Geometry, Statistics and Probability, and Grammar.

FROM STRESS TO SUCCESS

Watch *From Stress to Success*, a brief but insightful YouTube video that offers the tips, tricks, and secrets experts use to score higher on the exam.

REVIEWS

Leave a review, send us helpful feedback, or sign up for Cirrus's promotions—including free books!

To access these materials, please enter the following URL into your browser: **http://www.cirrustestprep.com/praxis-core-academic-skills-for-educators-online-resources.**

Introduction

Congratulations on choosing to take the Praxis Core Academic Skills for Educators Tests (5713, 5723, and 5733)! By purchasing this book, you've taken the first step toward becoming a teacher, an enriching and satisfying career.

This guide will provide you with a detailed overview of the Praxis Core Academic Skills for Educators Tests, also known as the Praxis Core Tests or Praxis Series, so you know exactly what to expect on test day. It will prepare you for all three of the Core Academic Skills for Educators tests: Reading (5713), Writing (5723), and Mathematics (5733). We'll take you through all the concepts covered on these tests and give you the opportunity to test your knowledge with practice questions. Even if it's been a while since you last took a major test, don't worry; we'll make sure you're more than ready!

WHAT IS THE PRAXIS CORE ACADEMIC SKILLS FOR EDUCATORS?

The Praxis Core Tests are used by teacher preparation programs in many states to measure applicants' aptitude in mathematics, reading, and writing. They are generally all required and may be referred to as the Praxis Series. You may take the tests individually on separate dates, or you may take them all on the same date by registering for the Praxis Core Academic Skills for Educators: Combined Test. In addition to its use as a determinant for entry into teaching programs, the Praxis Series is also used by many states to determine whether individuals receive teaching licenses. While there are other Praxis tests for specific academic subjects you may also be required to take, these core subjects are essential for anyone entering the teaching profession. Some states, however, require their own, independently created exam in lieu of the Praxis Series. It is important to check the specific requirements of *your* state to ensure you take the right exams.

What's on the Praxis Core Academic Skills for Educators?

The Praxis Core Tests gauge college-level skills in mathematics, reading, and writing in accordance with the Common Core State Standards. Each test—Reading, Writing, and Mathematics—is broken down into different categories based on the skills needed to succeed in a teacher preparation program.

On the Reading Test (5713) you will read and answer questions about fiction and nonfiction passages, which will be of varying length. Some will be paired. They may be taken from any reading material an educated adult is likely to encounter, including novels, newspapers, magazines, articles on current events, and visual representations.

The Writing Test (5723) tests your ability to analyze purpose, production, and types of text and your language and research skills. You will write two essays and answer multiple-choice questions.

The Mathematics Test (5733) focuses on numbers, data interpretation, statistics, algebra, and geometry. There may be more than one answer choice on some multiple-choice questions (these are designated with boxes rather than ovals or circles). A calculator will appear on screen when you are permitted to use one.

What's on the Praxis Core Academic Skills for Educators: Combined Test?			
Section	**Concepts**	**Number of Questions**	**Time**
Reading (5713)	Main idea and supporting details, text structure, and integration of ideas	56 multiple-choice questions following paired, long, and short passages and brief statements	85 minutes
Writing (5723)	Text types, purposes and production; language; research skills for writing	40 multiple-choice questions and 2 essays	40 minutes + 30 minutes each for each essay (100 minutes total)
Mathematics (5733)	Number and quantity; data interpretation and representation, statistics, and probability; algebra and geometry	56 multiple-choice and numeric entry questions	90 minutes

Section	Concepts	Number of Questions	Time
Total		152 (and 2 essays)	**5 hours is allotted in total for the combined test; 2 hours in total for each individual test if they are taken separately. Allotted time provides for tutorials and review of background information.**

HOW IS THE PRAXIS CORE ACADEMIC SKILLS FOR EDUCATORS SCORED?

Your scores become available 2 – 3 weeks after the exam on your online account; you will be notified via email when they are released. In most cases, your Praxis scores will automatically be sent to the credentialing agency of the state in which you test. In addition, when you register you may choose four recipient institutions for your scores; they will be sent directly for free. (If you complete or plan to complete a teacher preparation program in Guam, Maine, New Mexico, Texas, the US Virgin Islands, or Wisconsin, you *must* list your educational institution as a score recipient.) After your scores become available, you may send them to other institutions for an additional charge. Check http://www.ets.org to determine how this applies to your specific situation.

Each multiple-choice question is worth one raw point. The total number of questions you answer correctly is added up to obtain your raw score. Essay responses are scored on a holistic scale of 1 – 6 by two separate graders who are unaware of each other's evaluations of your work. Their scores are added together for a total of 2 – 12; if they differ substantially, to ensure fairness a third scorer determines your final essay score. This number is added to your raw score, which is then scaled to result in your final score.

Upon completion of the test, you will immediately receive an unofficial score report. Before receiving the report, however, you have the option to cancel your scores. You will receive your official score report 10 – 16 days after taking the exam.

Keep in mind that a small number of multiple-choice questions are experimental and will not count toward your overall score. ETS uses these to test out new questions for future exams. However, as those questions are not indicated on the test, you must respond to every question.

There is no penalty for guessing on the test, so be sure to eliminate answer choices and answer every question. If you still do not know the answer, guess; you may get it right!

How is the Praxis Core Academic Skills for Educators Administered?

The Praxis is a computer-based test offered continuously at a range of universities and testing centers. It may be taken in its individual parts or all at once. Check https://www.ets.org/praxis/register/centers_dates/ for more information. You will need to print your registration ticket from your online account and bring it, along with your identification, to the testing site on test day. No pens, pencils, erasers, or calculators are allowed; on the Mathematics portion of the exam, a calculator will automatically appear on the computer screen for certain questions. You may take the test once every 21 days.

About Cirrus Test Prep

Cirrus Test Prep study guides are designed by current and former educators and are tailored to meet your needs as an incoming educator. Our guides offer all of the resources necessary to help you pass teacher certification tests across the nation.

Cirrus clouds are graceful, wispy clouds characterized by their high altitude. Just like cirrus clouds, Cirrus Test Prep's goal is to help educators "aim high" when it comes to obtaining their teacher certification and entering the classroom.

About This Guide

This guide will help you master the most important test topics and also develop critical test-taking skills. We have built features into our books to prepare you for your tests and increase your score. Along with a detailed summary of the test's format, content, and scoring, we offer an in-depth overview of the content knowledge required to pass the test. Our sidebars provide interesting information, highlight key concepts, and review content so that you can solidify your understanding of the exam's concepts. Test your knowledge with sample questions and detailed answer explanations in the text that help you think through the problems on the exam and two full-length practice tests that reflect the content and format of the Praxis. We're pleased you've chosen Cirrus to be a part of your professional journey!

Reading Skills

INTRODUCTION

The Reading Test assesses overall proficiency in several key reading skills, including building inferences, understanding themes, and describing the organization and craft of writing.

The test has fifty-six multiple-choice questions. Questions follow a brief passage of text or media, such as a graph. The number of questions following each passage depends on how long the passage is: four to seven questions follow a 200-word passage or a pair of passages; three questions follow a 100-word passage; and single questions follow statements and briefer passages. Question stems may appear as fill-in-the-blank sentences, straightforward questions, or *LEAST/NEVER/EXCEPT* questions, which ask the reader to choose the answer that does not fit.

The Praxis Reading Test has three main question categories based on the Common Core State Standards. Several strategies and terms are discussed in the following sections and throughout this book.

KEY IDEAS AND DETAILS

This category focuses on the text as a whole. The questions ask for explanations of the main ideas and how they lead to inferences and conclusions. Look for connections between sections of the text as well as consistency and meaning of the author's argument. Test takers should also identify and accurately summarize the theme by giving details that support the author's argument.

Strategies for approaching this type of question include previewing the questions and outlining. Reading through the questions before reading the passage is a good way for students to find a focus. The questions describe what to look for, and students can rule out wrong answer choices by finding the main ideas and supporting details. Students can outline the text by jotting down words or phrases that describe the main idea of each paragraph and underlining important details that support that idea.

CRAFT, STRUCTURE, AND LANGUAGE SKILLS

This category tests understanding of the craft of writing. This includes the use of language, point of view, and organization. Questions may require relating the details of a passage to the overall organization and meaning of that passage. These questions ask for evaluations of specific areas of the text as they relate to the author's purpose and argument, and descriptions of how the author uses specific words, figurative language, or transitions.

For these craft-related questions, the best strategy entails returning to the passage after reading each question and looking for the specific context and location of each question. Marking wrong answers and circling the important aspects of the question stem and answer are also helpful strategies.

INTEGRATING KNOWLEDGE AND SKILLS

This final category combines the strategies used with the other two categories. The synthesis of these skills extends into evaluation and judgment.

Questions may require an assessment of a text, a comparison of multiple texts, or an examination of other kinds of texts, such as visual media. To compare two texts, for example, the test taker must understand the purpose and main idea of each text as well as specific details. Determining what to pay attention to is accomplished by reviewing each question before reading its relative passage and returning to the passage as needed. A passage with media such as visuals requires the same skills as reading text. Readers should consider each question to determine the skills and knowledge needed to answer it. Deconstructing the question stem reveals what sort of question it is.

THE MAIN IDEA

IDENTIFYING THE MAIN IDEA

The main idea of a text is the argument the author is making about a particular topic. Every sentence in a passage should support or address the main idea in some way. To identify the main idea, first identify the topic. The difference between the two is simple: the **topic** is the overall subject matter of a passage; the **main idea** is what the author wants to say about that topic.

Consider a political election. A candidate is running for office and plans to deliver a speech asserting her position on tax reform, which is that taxes should be lowered. The topic of the speech is tax reform, and the main idea is that taxes should be lowered. The candidate is going to say this in her speech and support it with examples proving why lowering taxes would benefit the public and how it could be accomplished.

Other candidates may have different perspectives on the same topic. They may think higher taxes are necessary or current taxes are adequate. Their speeches, while on the same topic of tax reform, would probably have different main ideas supported by different examples and evidence.

Read the following passage and identify the topic and main idea.

Babe Didrikson Zaharias, one of the most decorated female athletes of the twentieth century, is an inspiration for everyone. Born in 1911 in Beaumont, Texas, Zaharias lived in a time when women were considered second class to men, but she never let that stop her from becoming a champion. Zaharias was one of seven children in a poor immigrant family and was competitive from an early age. As a child she excelled at most things she tried, especially sports, which continued into high school and beyond. After high school, Zaharias played amateur basketball for two years, and soon after began training in track and field. Despite the fact that women were only allowed to enter in three events, Zaharias represented the United States in the 1932 Los Angeles Olympics, and won two gold medals and one silver in track and field events.

The topic of this paragraph is obviously Babe Zaharias—the whole passage describes events from her life. Determining the main idea, however, requires a little more analysis. To figure out the main idea, ask what the writer is saying about Zaharias. The writer describes Zaharias as an inspiration and talks about the hardships she overcame and her many accomplishments. These details support the writer's main idea: Babe Zaharias is an accomplished and inspirational woman.

Fictional works may have a theme instead of a main idea. A **theme** is an idea or perspective that emerges from the way a literary work engages with its topic. For example, a central topic in F. Scott Fitzgerald's novel *The Great Gatsby* is money: the characters are all defined by their relative wealth. The theme of the novel is what Fitzgerald is trying to say about money: that being extremely wealthy leads to excess and moral decay.

SAMPLE QUESTIONS

The Battle of the Little Bighorn, commonly called Custer's Last Stand, was a battle between the Lakota, the Northern Cheyenne, the Arapaho, and the Seventh Cavalry Regiment of the US Army. Led by war leaders Crazy Horse and Chief Gall and the religious leader Sitting Bull, the allied tribes of the Plains Indians decisively defeated their US foes. Two hundred and sixty-eight US soldiers were killed, including General George Armstrong Custer, two of his brothers, his nephew, his brother-in-law, and six Indian scouts.

1) **What is the main idea of this passage?**

    A.   Most of General Custer's family died in the Battle of the Little Bighorn.

    B.   Crazy Horse and Chief Gall were important leaders of the Plains Indians.

    C.   The Seventh Cavalry Regiment was formed to fight Native American tribes.

    D.   Sitting Bull and George Custer were fierce enemies.

    E.   The Battle of the Little Bighorn was a significant victory for the Plains Indians.

In 1953, doctors surgically removed the hippocampus of patient Henry Molaison in an attempt to stop his frequent seizures. Unexpectedly, he lost the ability to form new memories, leading to the biggest breakthrough in the science of memory. Molaison's long-term memory—of events more than a year before his surgery—was unchanged, as was his ability to learn physical skills. From this, scientists learned that different types of memory are handled by different parts of the brain, with the hippocampus responsible for *episodic memory*, the short-term recall of events. They have since discovered that some memories are then channeled to the cortex, the outer layers of the brain that handle higher functions, where they are gradually integrated with related information to build lasting knowledge about our world.

2) **The main idea of the passage is that**

    A.   Molaison's surgery posed significant risk to the functioning of his brain.

    B.   short-term and long-term memory are stored in different parts of the brain.

    C.   long-term memory forms over a longer period than short-term memory.

    D.   memories of physical skills are processed differently than memories of events.

    E.   the hippocampus stores all memories related to events.

Topic and Summary Sentences

The topic, and sometimes the main idea of a paragraph, is introduced in the **topic sentence**. The topic sentence usually appears early in a passage. The first sentence in the paragraph about Babe Zaharias states the topic and main idea: "Babe Didrikson Zaharias, one of the most decorated female athletes of the twentieth century, is an inspiration for everyone."

Even though paragraphs generally begin with topic sentences, writers sometimes build up to the topic sentence by using supporting details to generate interest or build an argument. Readers should watch out for paragraphs that do not include a clear topic sentence.

The **summary sentence**, on the other hand, often—but not always—comes at the end of a paragraph or passage, because it wraps up all the ideas presented. This sentence provides an understanding of what the author wants to say about the topic and what conclusions to draw about it.

The topic sentence acts as an introduction to a topic, allowing readers to activate their own ideas and experiences. The summary statement asks readers to accept the author's ideas about that topic. A summary sentence helps readers quickly identify a piece's main idea.

SAMPLE QUESTIONS

The Constitution of the United States establishes a series of limits to rein in centralized power. "Separation of powers" distributes federal authority among three branches: the executive, the legislative, and the judicial. The system of "checks and balances" prevents any one branch from usurping power. "States' rights" are protected under the Constitution from too much encroachment by the federal government. "Enumeration of powers" names the specific and few powers the federal government has. These four restrictions have helped sustain the American republic for over two centuries.

3) **Which of the following is the passage's topic sentence?**

   A. These four restrictions have helped sustain the American republic for over two centuries.

   B. The Constitution of the United States establishes a series of limits to rein in centralized power.

   C. "Enumeration of powers" names the specific and few powers the federal government has.

   D. The system of "checks and balances" prevents any one branch from usurping power.

   E. "Separation of powers" distributes federal authority among three branches: the executive, the legislative, and the judicial.

4) **Which of the following is the passage's summary sentence?**

   A. These four restrictions have helped sustain the American republic for over two centuries.

   B. The Constitution of the United States establishes a series of limits to rein in centralized power.

   C. "Enumeration of powers" names the specific and few powers the federal government has.

   D. The system of "checks and balances" prevents any one branch from usurping power.

   E. "Separation of powers" distributes federal authority among three branches: the executive, the legislative, and the judicial.

SUPPORTING DETAILS

The middle of a paragraph is built with **supporting details**. Supporting details come in many forms. The purpose of the passage dictates the type of details that will support the main idea. A persuasive passage may use facts and data or give specific reasons for the author's opinion. An informative passage will mostly use facts about the topic to support the main idea. Even a narrative passage will have supporting details—specific things the author says to develop the story and characters.

The most important aspect of supporting details is that they support the main idea. Examining supporting details and how they work together will help readers understand the author's view on a topic and the passage's main idea. Supporting details are key to understanding a passage.

How can readers identify the most important information in a passage? Supporting details help pinpoint the main idea, but it is easier to first locate the most important supporting details by understanding the main idea. This way, the pieces that make up the main argument become clear.

Let's look again at the passage about athlete Babe Zaharias.

> Babe Didrikson Zaharias, one of the most decorated female athletes of the twentieth century, is an inspiration for everyone. Born in 1911 in Beaumont, Texas, Zaharias lived in a time when women were considered second class to men, but she never let that stop her from becoming a champion. Babe was one of seven children in a poor immigrant family and was competitive from an early age. As a child she excelled at most things she tried, especially sports, which continued into high school and beyond. After high school, Babe played amateur basketball for two years, and soon after began training in track and field. Despite the fact that women were only allowed to enter in three events, Zaharias represented the United States in the 1932 Los Angeles Olympics, and won two gold medals and one silver for track and field events.

The main idea is that Zaharias is someone to admire—an idea introduced in the opening sentence. The rest of the paragraph gives details that support this idea. These details include the circumstances of her childhood, her early success at sports, and the medals she won at the Olympics.

Readers looking for supporting details should watch for signal words. **Signal words** are transitions and conjunctions that explain how one sentence or idea is connected to another. They "signal" that a supporting fact or idea will follow, and so can be helpful in identifying supporting details. These words and phrases can be anywhere in a sentence. Signal words can add information, provide counterarguments, create organization in a passage, or draw conclusions. Some common signal words are "in particular," "in addition," "besides," "in contrast," "therefore," and "because."

Signal words can also help rule out certain sentences as the main idea or topic sentence. If a sentence begins with one of these phrases, it will likely be too specific to be a main idea.

Readers can use supporting details to understand the main idea of a text or support an argument, but they must evaluate these details for relevance and consistency. The author might leave out details that do not directly support the main idea of a text or that support an opposing argument. Readers should think critically about what information authors choose to include or leave out. This is particularly important in persuasive writing, when an author's bias may influence their writing.

Critical reading means being alert for striking features of a text. For example, does a description seem exaggerated or overstated? Do certain words—such as "agonizing"—seem overly emotive? Are rhetorical questions used to lead the reader to a certain conclusion? Bias and audience are discussed later in this chapter (see "Understanding the Author" on page 11).

SAMPLE QUESTIONS

For thirteen years, a spacecraft called *Cassini* was on an exploratory mission to Saturn. The spacecraft was designed not to return but to end its journey by diving into Saturn's atmosphere. This dramatic ending provided scientists with unprecedented information about Saturn's atmosphere and its magnetic and gravitational fields. First, however, *Cassini* passed Saturn's largest moon, Titan, where it recorded data on Titan's curious methane lakes, gathering information about potential seasons on the planet-sized moon. Then it passed through the unexplored region between Saturn itself and its famous rings. Scientists hope to learn how old the rings are and to directly examine the particles that make them up. *Cassini*'s mission ended in 2017, but researchers have new questions for future exploration.

5) **According to the passage, scientists want to learn more about Titan's**

    A.   gravity, based on examination of its magnetic field.

    B.   rings, based on the particles that compose them.

    C.   seasons, based on changes to its lakes.

    D.   age, based on analysis of its minerals and gases.

    E.   atmosphere, based on measurements of its gravity.

The study showed that private tutoring gives a significant advantage to those students who are able to afford it. Researchers looked at the grades of students who had received free tutoring through the school versus those whose parents had paid for private tutors. The study included 2500 students in three high schools across four grade levels. The study found that private tutoring corresponded with a rise in grade point average (GPA) of 0.5 compared to students who used the school's free tutor service, and 0.7 compared to students who used no tutoring. After reviewing the study, the board is recommending that the school restructure its free tutor service to provide a more equitable education for all students.

6)   **Which of the following would weaken the author's argument?**

     A.   the fact that the cited study was funded by a company that provides discounted tutoring through schools

     B.   a study showing differences in standardized test scores between students at schools in different neighborhoods

     C.   a statement signed by local teachers stating that they do not provide preferential treatment in the classroom or when grading

     D.   a study showing that GPA does not strongly correlate with success in college

     E.   a pricing schedule for private tutors who provided services to students in the study

Facts and Opinions

A **fact** is a piece of information that can be proven true or false. Its truthfulness or falsity cannot be changed, no matter who verifies it. The statement "Wednesday comes after Tuesday" is a fact—anyone can point to a calendar to prove it. An **opinion** is a belief that others may or may not agree with. The assertion "Television is more entertaining than feature films" is an opinion—people will agree or disagree with this statement, and there is no reference to prove or disprove it.

Authors use both facts and opinions as supporting details. They may mix facts with opinions or state an opinion as if it were a fact. The exam may ask readers to differentiate between facts and opinions.

> **QUICK REVIEW**
>
> Choose the phrase that signals an opinion: "for example," "studies have shown," "I believe," "in fact," "it is possible that."

SAMPLE QUESTION

The most important part of brewing coffee is getting the right water. Choose a water that you think has a nice, neutral flavor. Anything with too many minerals or contaminants will change the flavor of the coffee, and water with too few minerals won't do a good job of extracting the flavor from the coffee beans. Water should be heated to between 195 and 205 degrees Fahrenheit. Boiling water (212 degrees Fahrenheit) will burn the beans and give your coffee a scorched flavor.

While the water is heating, grind your beans. Remember, the fresher the grind, the fresher the flavor of the coffee. The number of beans depends on your personal taste. Obviously, more beans will result in a more robust flavor, while fewer beans will give your coffee a more subtle taste. The texture of the grind should not be too fine (which can lead to bitter coffee) or too coarse (which can lead to weak coffee).

Once the beans are ground and the water has reached the perfect temperature, you're ready to brew. A French press (which we recommend) allows you to control brewing time and provide a thorough brew. Pour the grounds into the press, then pour the hot water over the grounds and let it steep. The brew shouldn't require more than five minutes, although if you like your coffee a bit harsher, you can leave it longer. Finally, use the plunger to remove the grounds and pour.

7) **Which of the following statements based on the passage should be considered an opinion?**

A. While the water is heating, grind your beans.

B. A French press (which we recommend) allows you to control brewing time and provide a thorough brew.

C. Anything with too many minerals or contaminants will change the flavor of the coffee, and water with too few minerals won't do a good job of extracting the flavor from the coffee beans.

D. Finally, use the plunger to remove the grounds and pour.

E. Obviously, more beans will result in a more robust flavor, while fewer beans will give your coffee a more subtle taste.

MAKING INFERENCES

In addition to understanding the main idea and factual content of a passage, readers should think about other information in a passage. In a nonfiction passage, for example, questions might ask which statement the author would agree with. In a fictional work, readers might be asked to anticipate what a character would do next.

To answer such questions, readers need to understand the topic and main idea of the passage. This information allows the reader to figure out which of the answer choices best fits the criteria (or, alternatively, which do not).

Readers should try to understand the explicit meanings of information or a narrative. This happens when they draw conclusions and make logical inferences. To draw a conclusion, readers consider the details or facts. They then come to a **conclusion**—the next logical point in the thought sequence.

For example, in a Hemingway story, an old man sits alone in a café. A young waiter says that the café is closing, but the old man continues to drink. The waiter starts closing up, and the old man signals for a refill. Based on these details, the reader might conclude that the old man has not understood the waiter's desire for him to leave.

> **HELPFUL HINT**
>
> Readers draw conclusions by thinking about how the author wants them to feel. Some carefully selected facts can cause readers to feel a certain way.

An inference is different from a conclusion. An **inference** is an assumption the reader makes based on details in the text as well as their own knowledge. It is more of an educated guess that extends the literal meaning. Inferences begin with the given details. The reader then uses these to figure out more facts. What the reader already knows informs what is suggested by the details of decisions or situations in the text. In the example above, the reader might infer that the old man is lonely, enjoys being in the café, and is reluctant to leave.

It is important to infer character motivation when reading fictional text. The characters' actions move the plot forward. A series of events is understood by making sense of why the characters did what they did. Hemingway includes contrasting details as the young waiter and an older waiter discuss the old man. The older waiter sympathizes with the old man. Both men have no one at home and experience a sense of emptiness in life, which brings them to the café.

DID YOU KNOW?

When considering a character's motivations, the reader should ask what the character wants to achieve, what the character will get by accomplishing this, and what the character seems to value the most.

Another aspect of understanding text is connecting it to other texts. Readers may connect the Hemingway story about the old man in the café to other Hemingway stories about people dealing with loss and loneliness in a dignified way. They can extend their initial connections to people they know or their personal experiences.

When readers read a persuasive text, they often connect the arguments made to counterarguments and opposing evidence of which they are aware. They use these connections to infer meaning.

SAMPLE QUESTIONS

Between November 15 and December 21, 1864, Major General William Tecumseh Sherman marched Union troops from the recently captured city of Atlanta to the port of Savannah. The goal was not only to capture the port city and secure Georgia for the Union but also to destroy the Confederacy's infrastructure and demoralize its people. Sherman and his troops destroyed rail lines and burned buildings and fields. They packed only twenty days' worth of rations, foraging for the rest of their supplies from farms along the way. By the time they reached Savannah, they had destroyed 300 miles of railroad and countless cotton gins and mills, and seized 4000 mules, 13,000 head of cattle, 9.5 million pounds of corn, and 10.5 million pounds of fodder. Sherman estimated his troops inflicted $100 million in damages.

8) **It can be inferred from the passage that the Confederacy**
   A. strongly resisted the actions of Sherman's troops.
   B. was greatly weakened by the destruction.
   C. used the march as a rallying point.
   D. was relatively unaffected by the march.
   E. relied heavily on the port of Savannah.

The cisco, a foot-long freshwater fish native to the Great Lakes, once thrived throughout the basin but had virtually disappeared by the 1950s. Today, however, fishermen are pulling them up by the net-load in Lake Michigan and Lake Ontario. It is highly unusual for a native species to revive, and the reason for the cisco's reemergence is even more unlikely. The cisco have an invasive species, quagga mussels, to thank for their return. Quagga mussels depleted nutrients in the lakes, harming other species highly dependent on these nutrients. Cisco, however, thrive in low-nutrient environments. As other species—many invasive—diminished, cisco flourished in their place.

9)   It can be inferred from the passage that most invasive species

    A.   support the growth of native species.

    B.   do not impact the development of native species.

    C.   struggle to survive in their new environments.

    D.   cause the decline of native species.

    E.   compete with each other for resources.

UNDERSTANDING THE AUTHOR

Many questions on the Praxis Reading Test will ask readers to interpret an author's intentions and ideas. This means readers must examine the author's perspective and purpose as well as the way the author uses language to communicate these things.

In every passage, an author chooses words, structures, and content with specific purpose and intent. With this in mind, the reader can understand why an author picks certain words and structures and how these relate to the content.

THE AUTHOR'S PURPOSE

The author sets out with a specific goal: to communicate a particular idea to an audience. The **author's purpose** is determined by asking why the author wants the reader to understand the passage's main idea. There are four purposes an author might have:

▶   to entertain the reader

▶   to persuade the reader of an opinion or argument

▶   to describe something, such as a person, place, thing, or event

▶   to explain a process or procedure

Within each of these general purposes, the author may direct the audience to take a clear action or respond in a certain way.

Identifying an author's purpose can be tricky, but the writing itself often gives clues. For example, if an author's purpose is to entertain, the writing may include vivid characters, exciting plot twists, or beautiful, figurative language. On the other hand, if an author wishes to persuade the reader, there may be an argument or convincing examples that support the author's point of view. An author who wishes to describe a person, place, or event may include lots of details as well as plenty of adjectives and adverbs. Finally, the author whose purpose is to explain a process or procedure may include step-by-step instructions or information in a sequence.

There are different **modes** of written materials that are related to an author's purpose. A short story, for example, is meant to entertain, while an online news article is designed to inform the public about a current event. Each type of writing has a specific name:

▶ Narrative writing tells a story (novel, short story, play).

▶ Informational or expository writing informs people (newspaper and magazine articles).

▶ Technical writing explains something (product manual, instructions).

▶ Persuasive writing tries to convince the reader of something (opinion column or a blog).

The author's purpose for writing a passage is also connected to the structure of that text. In a **narrative**, the author tells a story to illustrate a theme or idea the reader needs to consider. In a narrative, the author uses characteristics of story-telling, such as chronological order, characters, and a defined setting, and these characteristics communicate the author's theme or main idea.

In an **expository** passage, on the other hand, the author simply seeks to explain an idea or topic to the reader. The main idea will probably be a factual statement or a direct assertion of a broadly held opinion. Expository writing can come in many forms, but one essential feature is a fair and balanced representation of a topic. The author may explore one detailed aspect or a broad range of characteristics, but he or she mainly seeks to prompt a decision from the reader.

Similarly, in **technical** writing, the author's purpose is to explain specific processes, techniques, or equipment so the reader can use that process or equipment to get a desired result. Writing like this uses chronological or spatial structures, specialized vocabulary, and imperative or directive language.

> **TEACHING TIP**
>
> When reading a persuasive text, students should be aware of what the author believes about the topic.

In **persuasive** writing, the author seeks to convince the reader to accept an opinion or belief. Much like expository writing, persuasive writing is presented in many organizational forms, but the author uses specific techniques, or **rhetorical strategies**, to build an argument. Readers can identify these strategies to clearly understand what an author wants them to believe, how the author's perspective and purpose may lead to bias, and whether the passage includes any logical fallacies.

Common rhetorical strategies include the appeals to ethos, logos, and pathos. An author uses these to build trust with the reader, to explain the logical points of their argument, and to convince the reader to agree with their opinion.

An **ethos—ethical—appeal** uses balanced, fair language and seeks to build a trusting relationship between the author and the reader. An author might explain their credentials, include the reader in an argument, or offer concessions to an opposing argument.

A **logos—logical—appeal** builds on that trust by providing facts and support for the author's opinion, explaining the argument with clear connections and reasoning. At this point, the reader should beware of logical fallacies that connect unrelated ideas and build arguments on faulty premises. With a logical appeal, an author tries to convince the reader to accept an opinion or belief by showing that not only is it the most logical option, but it also satisfies the reader's emotional reaction to a topic.

A **pathos—emotional—appeal** does not depend on reasonable connections between ideas. Instead, it reminds the reader, through imagery, strong language, and personal connections, that the author's argument aligns with the reader's best interests.

Many persuasive passages use all three rhetorical strategies to appeal to the reader.

Clues will help the reader determine many things about a passage, from the author's purpose to the passage's main idea, but understanding an author's purpose is essential to fully understanding the text.

SAMPLE QUESTIONS

The Gatling gun, a forerunner of the modern machine gun, was an early rapid-fire spring-loaded, hand-cranked weapon. In 1861, Dr. Richard J. Gatling designed the gun to allow one person to fire many shots quickly. His goal was to reduce the death toll of war by decreasing the number of soldiers needed to fight. The gun had a central shaft surrounded by six rotating barrels. A soldier turned a crank, which rotated the shaft. As each barrel reached a particular point in the cycle, it fired, ejected its spent cartridge, and loaded another. During this process, it cooled down, preparing it to fire again. The Gatling gun was first used in combat by the Union Army during the Civil War. However, each gun was purchased directly by individual commanders. The US Army did not purchase a Gatling gun until 1866.

10) **The primary purpose of the passage is to**

A. explain why the Gatling gun was harmful to troops.

B. critique the US Army's use of the Gatling gun.

C. describe the design and early history of the Gatling gun.

D. analyze the success of Dr. Gatling in achieving his goals.

E. compare the Gatling gun to the modern machine gun.

The greatest changes in sensory, motor, and perceptual development happen in the first two years of life. When babies are first born, most of their senses operate in a similar way to those of adults. For example, babies are able to hear before they are born. Studies show that babies turn toward the sound of their mothers' voices just minutes after being born, indicating they recognize the mother's voice from their time in the womb.

The exception to this is vision. A baby's vision changes significantly in the first year of life. Infants initially have a range of vision of only 8 – 12 inches and no depth perception. As a result, they rely primarily on hearing. Vision does not become the dominant sense until babies are around twelve months old. Babies prefer faces to other objects. This preference, along with their limited vision range, means that their sight is initially focused on their caregiver.

11) **Which of the following best describes the mode of the passage?**
    A.   expository
    B.   narrative
    C.   persuasive
    D.   descriptive
    E.   rhetorical

Text Structure

The structure of a text determines how the reader understands the argument and how the various details interact to form the argument. Authors can structure passages in several different ways. These distinct organizational patterns, referred to as **text structure**, use the logical relationships between ideas to improve the readability and coherence of a text. The most common ways passages are organized are:

▶   **problem-solution**: The author outlines a problem and then discusses a solution.

▶   **comparison-contrast**: The author presents two situations and then discusses the similarities and differences.

▶   **cause-effect**: The author recounts an action and then discusses the resulting effects.

▶   **descriptive**: The author describes an idea, object, person, or other item in detail.

▶   **chronological**: The author describes a situation or tells a story in chronological order.

HELPFUL HINT

Authors often use repetition to reinforce an idea, including repeated words, phrases, or images.

When analyzing a text, the reader should consider how text structure influences the author's meaning. Most important, the reader needs to be aware of how an author emphasizes an idea by the way he or she presents information. For example, including a contrasting idea makes a central idea stand out, and including a series of concrete examples creates a force of facts to support an argument.

SAMPLE QUESTION

The greatest changes in sensory, motor, and perceptual development happen in the first two years of life. When babies are first born, most of their senses operate in a similar way to those of adults. For example, babies are able to hear before they are born. Studies show that babies turn toward the sound of their mothers' voices just minutes after being born, indicating they recognize the mother's voice from their time in the womb.

The exception to this is vision. A baby's vision changes significantly in the first year of life. Infants initially have a range of vision of only 8 – 12 inches and no depth perception. As a result, they rely primarily on hearing. Vision does not become the dominant sense until babies are around twelve months old. Babies prefer faces to other objects. This preference, along with their limited vision range, means that their sight is initially focused on their caregiver.

12) **Which term BEST describes the structure of the text?**

    A.   chronological

    B.   cause-effect

    C.   problem-solution

    D.   comparison-contrast

    E.   descriptive

THE AUDIENCE

The structure, purpose, main idea, and language of a text all converge on one target: the intended audience. An author makes decisions about every aspect of a piece of writing based on that audience, and readers evaluate the writing through the lens of that audience.

By considering the likely reactions of an intended audience, readers can determine many things: whether they are part of that intended audience; the author's purpose for using specific techniques or devices; the biases of the author and how they appear in the writing; and how the author uses rhetorical strategies. While readers evaluate each of these things separately, identifying and considering the intended audience deepens a reader's understanding of a text and helps highlight details.

Readers can figure out a text's intended audience by asking a few questions. First, what is the main idea of the passage? Who most likely cares about that idea, benefits from it, or needs to know about it? Answering those questions will help reveal the intended audience. For example, if the main idea of a passage is "signs you need to take your car to the mechanic," the audience is probably car owners who do not have a lot of technical knowledge.

> **QUICK REVIEW**
>
> A logical argument includes a claim, a reason that supports the claim, and an assumption the reader makes based on accepted beliefs. All parts of the argument need to make sense to the reader, so authors often consider their audience's beliefs as they make their arguments.

Then the reader considers language. The author tailors language to appeal to the intended audience. Readers can understand the audience based on the type of language used. For example, the figurative language John Steinbeck uses in his novel *The Grapes of Wrath* describes the suffering of Americans who migrated to California to find work during the Great Depression of the 1930s.

Steinbeck spoke directly to the Americans who were discriminating against the migrants. Instead of finding work in the "land of milk and honey," migrants faced poverty and injustice. The metaphor that gives the novel its title is "and in the eyes of the people there is the failure; and in the eyes of the hungry there is a growing wrath. In the souls of the people the grapes of wrath are filling and growing heavy, growing heavy for the vintage." Steinbeck used the image of ripening grapes, familiar to those surrounded by vineyards, to condemn the harsh treatment of impoverished migrants and inspire compassion in his audience.

SAMPLE QUESTION

The social and political discourse of America continues to be permeated with idealism. An idealistic viewpoint asserts that the ideals of freedom, equality, justice, and human dignity are the truths that Americans must continue to aspire to. Idealists argue that truth is what should be, not necessarily what is. In general, they work to improve things and to make them as close to ideal as possible.

13) **Which phrase BEST describes the author's purpose?**

   A.   to advocate for freedom, equality, justice, and human rights

   B.   to explain what an idealist believes in

   C.   to explain what's wrong with social and political discourse in America

   D.   to persuade readers to believe in certain truths

   E.   to encourage readers to question the truth

TONE AND MOOD

The **tone** of a passage describes the author's attitude toward the topic. The **mood** is the main feeling or atmosphere in a passage that provokes specific emotions in the reader. The subtle distinction between these two aspects lies in the audience: the mood influences the reader's emotional state in response to the piece, while the tone establishes a relationship between the audience and the author. Does the author want to instruct the audience? Is the author more experienced than the audience? Does the author wish to convey a friendly or equal relationship? In each of these cases, the author uses a different tone to reflect the desired level of communication.

TEACHING TIP

To determine the author's tone, students should examine what overall feeling they are experiencing.

Diction, or word choice, primarily determines mood and tone in a passage. Many readers use only an author's ideas to determine tone. It is better to find specific words from the text and look for patterns in connotation and emotion. By considering categories of words used by the author, the reader can discover the overall emotional atmosphere of a text and the author's attitude toward the subject.

Every word has both a literal meaning and a **connotative meaning**. The latter relies on the common emotions, associations, and experiences an audience might associate with that word. The following words are all synonyms: "dog," "puppy," "cur," "mutt," "canine," "pet." Two of these words—"dog" and "canine"—are neutral words, without strong associations or emotions. Two others—"pet" and "puppy"—have positive associations. The last two—"cur" and "mutt"—have negative associations. A passage that uses one pair of these words versus another pair activates the positive or negative reactions of the audience.

HELPFUL HINT

To determine the connotation of a word, the reader examines whether it conveys a positive or negative association. Adjectives are often used to influence the reader's feelings, as in the phrase "an ambitious attempt to achieve."

SAMPLE QUESTIONS

Alan—

I just wanted to drop you a quick note to let you know I'll be out of the office for the next two weeks. Elizabeth and I are finally taking that trip to France we've been talking about for years. It's a bit of a last-minute decision, but since we had the vacation time available, we figured it was now or never.

Anyway, my team's been briefed on the upcoming meeting, so they should be able to handle the presentation without any hiccups. If you have any questions or concerns, you can direct them to Joanie, who'll be handling my responsibilities while I'm out.

Let me know if you want any special treats. I don't know if you can take chocolate and cheese on the plane, but I'm going to try!

Best regards,

Michael

14) **Which word BEST describes the relationship between the author and Alan?**
   A. familial
   B. formal
   C. friendly
   D. strained
   E. intimate

15) **Which phrase BEST captures the author's purpose?**
   A. to ask Alan if he wants any special treats from France
   B. to brag to Alan about his upcoming vacation
   C. to inform Alan that he will be out of the office
   D. to help Alan prepare for the upcoming meeting
   E. to introduce Alan to Joanie

MEANING OF WORDS AND PHRASES

Some questions on the exam may ask about the definitions or intended meanings of words within passages. Even if some of these words are new, there are tricks readers can use to figure out what they mean.

CONTEXT CLUES

Vocabulary-in-context questions ask about the meaning of specific words in the passage. The questions will ask which answer choice is most similar in meaning to the specified word, or which answer choice could be substituted for that word in the passage.

The passage itself can help clarify the meaning of unfamiliar words. Often, identifying the tone or main idea of the passage can help eliminate answer choices. For example, if the tone of the passage is generally positive, try eliminating the answer choices with a negative connotation. Or, if the passage is about a particular occupation, rule out words unrelated to that topic.

Passages may also provide specific **context clues** that can help determine the meaning of a word. One type of context clue is a **definition**, or **description**, **clue**. These are also known as **restatement clues**. The definition is often set apart from the rest of the sentence by a comma, parentheses, or a colon.

Sometimes authors use a difficult word, then include "that is" or "which is" to signal that they are giving a definition. An author also may use a synonym or restate the idea in more familiar words:

> Teachers often prefer teaching students with intrinsic motivation; these students have an internal desire to learn.

The meaning of "intrinsic" is restated as "internal."

Similarly, authors may include an **example clue**, using an example phrase that clarifies the meaning of the word:

> Carly found that yoga was efficacious for the cramping in her leg; the morning after yoga practice, her leg pain was gone.

"Efficacious," which means "effective," is explained with an example showing that yoga resolved the cramping in Carly's leg.

Another commonly used context clue is the **contrast**, or **antonym**, **clue**. In this case, authors indicate that the unfamiliar word is the opposite of a familiar word:

> In contrast to intrinsic motivation, extrinsic motivation is contingent on teachers offering rewards that are appealing.

The phrase "in contrast" tells the reader that "extrinsic" is the opposite of "intrinsic."

Positive/negative clues indicate whether a word has a positive or negative meaning:

> The film was lauded by critics as stunning and
> was nominated for several awards.

The positive descriptions "stunning" and "nominated for several awards" suggest that "lauded" has a positive meaning.

SAMPLE QUESTIONS

16) **Based on context clues, which word is closest in meaning to "incentivize" as used in the following sentence?**

    One challenge of teaching is finding ways to incentivize, or to motivate, learning.
    A.   encourage
    B.   determine
    C.   challenge
    D.   improve
    E.   dissuade

17) **Based on context clues, which word is closest in meaning to "apprehensive" as used in the following sentence?**

    If an extrinsic reward is extremely desirable, a student may become so apprehensive he or she cannot focus. The student may experience such intense pressure to perform that the reward undermines its intent.
    A.   uncertain
    B.   distracted
    C.   anxious
    D.   forgetful
    E.   resentful

WORD STRUCTURE

In addition to the context of a sentence or passage, an unfamiliar word itself can give the reader clues about its meaning. Each word has separate pieces that determine meaning. The most familiar of these pieces are word roots, prefixes, and suffixes.

Word roots are the bases from which many words take their form and meaning. The most common word roots are Greek and Latin, and a broad knowledge of these roots can greatly improve a reader's ability to determine the meaning of words in context. The root of a word does not always point to the word's exact meaning, but combined with an understanding of the word's place in a sentence and the context of a passage, it will often be enough to answer a question about meaning or relationships.

Table 1.1. Common Word Roots

Root	Meaning	Examples
alter	other	alternate, alter ego
ambi	both	ambidextrous
ami, amic	love	amiable
amphi	both ends, all sides	amphibian
anthrop	man, human, humanity	misanthrope, anthropologist
apert	open	aperture
aqua	water	aqueduct, aquarium
aud	to hear	audience
auto	self	autobiography
bell	war	belligerent, bellicose
bene	good	benevolent
bio	life	biology
ced	yield, go	secede, intercede
cent	one hundred	century
chron	time	chronological
circum	around	circumference
contra, counter	against	contradict
crac, crat	rule, ruler	autocrat, bureaucrat
crypt	hidden	cryptogram, cryptic
curr, curs, cours	to run	precursory
dict	to say	dictator, dictation
dyna	power	dynamic
dys	bad, hard, unlucky	dysfunctional
equ	equal, even	equanimity
fac	to make, to do	factory
form	shape	reform, conform
fort	strength	fortitude
fract	to break	fracture
grad, gress	step	progression
gram	thing written	epigram
graph	writing	graphic
hetero	different	heterogeneous
homo	same	homogenous
hypo	below, beneath	hypothermia

Root	Meaning	Examples
iso	identical	isometric
ject	throw	projection
logy	study of	biology
luc	light	elucidate
mal	bad	malevolent
meta, met	behind, between	metacognition
meter, metr	measure	thermometer
micro	small	microbe
mis, miso	hate	misanthrope
mit	to send	transmit
mono	one	monologue
morph	form, shape	morphology
mort	death	mortal
multi	many	multiple
phil	love	philanthropist
port	carry	transportation
pseudo	false	pseudonym
psycho	soul, spirit	psychic
rupt	to break	disruption
scope	viewing instrument	microscope
scrib, scribe	to write	inscription
sect, sec	to cut	section
sequ, secu	follow	consecutive
soph	wisdom, knowledge	philosophy
spect	to look	spectator
struct	to build	restructure
tele	far off	telephone
terr	earth	terrestrial
therm	heat	thermal
vent, vene	to come	convene
vert	turn	vertigo
voc	voice, call	vocalize, evocative

In addition to understanding the base of a word, readers should recognize common affixes that change the meaning of words and show their relationships to other words. **Prefixes** are added to the beginning of words and can change their meaning, sometimes to an opposite meaning.

Table 1.2. Common Prefixes

Prefix	Meaning	Examples
a, an	without, not	anachronism, anhydrous
ab, abs, a	apart, away from	abscission, abnormal
ad	toward	adhere
agere	act	agent
amphi, ambi	round, both sides	ambivalent
ante	before	antedate, anterior
anti	against	antipathy
archos	leader, first, chief	oligarchy
bene	well, favorable	benevolent, beneficent
bi	two	binary, bivalve
caco	bad	cacophony
circum	around	circumnavigate
corpus	body	corporeal
credo	belief	credible
demos	people	demographic
di	two, double	dimorphism, diatomic
dia	across, through	dialectic
dis	not, apart	disenfranchise
dyna	be able	dynamo, dynasty
ego	I, self	egomaniac, egocentric
epi	upon, over	epigram, epiphyte
ex	out	extraneous, extemporaneous
geo	earth	geocentric, geomancy
ideo	idea	ideology, ideation
ig, im	not	ignoble, immoral
in	in	induction, indigenous
inter	between	interstellar
lexis	word	lexicography
liber	free, book	liberal
locus	place	locality
macro	large	macrophage
micro	small	micron

Prefix	Meaning	Examples
mono	one, single	monocle, monovalent
mortis	death	moribund
olig	few	oligarchy
peri	around	peripatetic, perineum
poly	many	polygamy
pre	before	prescient
solus	alone	solitary
subter	under, secret	subterfuge
un	not	unsafe
utilis	useful	utilitarian

Suffixes are added to the end of words. They generally point out a word's relationship to other words in a sentence. Suffixes might change a part of speech or indicate if a word is plural or related to a plural.

Table 1.3. Common Suffixes

Suffix	Meaning	Examples
able, ible	able, capable	visible
age	act of, state of, result of	wreckage
al	relating to	gradual
algia	pain	myalgia
an, ian	native of, relating to	riparian
ance, ancy	action, process, state	defiance
ary, ery, ory	relating to, quality, place	aviary
cian	processing a specific skill or art	physician
cule, ling	very small	sapling, animalcule
cy	action, function	normalcy
dom	quality, realm	wisdom
ee	one who receives the action	nominee
en	made of, to make	silken
ence, ency	action, state of, quality	urgency
er, or	one who, that which	professor
escent	in the process of	adolescent, senescence
esis, osis	action, process, condition	genesis, neurosis
et, ette	small one, group	baronet, lorgnette
fic	making, causing	specific

Table 1.3. Common Suffixes (continued)

Suffix	Meaning	Examples
ful	full of	frightful
hood	order, condition, quality	adulthood
ice	condition, state, quality	malice
id, ide	connected with, belonging to	bromide
ile	relating to, suited for, capable of	puerile, juvenile
ine	nature of	feminine
ion, sion, tion	act, result, state of	contagion
ish	origin, nature, resembling	impish
ism	system, manner, condition, characteristic	capitalism
ist	one who, that which	artist, flautist
ite	nature of, quality of, mineral product	graphite
ity, ty	state of, quality	captivity
ive	causing, making	exhaustive
ize, ise	make	idolize, bowdlerize
ment	act of, state of, result	containment
nomy	law	autonomy, taxonomy
oid	resembling	asteroid, anthropoid
some	like, apt, tending to	gruesome
strat	cover	strata
tude	state of, condition of	aptitude
um	forms single nouns	spectrum
ure	state of, act, process, rank	rupture, rapture
ward	in the direction of	backward
y	inclined to, tend to	faulty

SAMPLE QUESTIONS

In December of 1945, Germany launched its last major offensive campaign of World War II, pushing through the dense forests of the Ardennes region of Belgium, France, and Luxembourg. The attack, designed to block the Allies from the Belgian port of Antwerp and to split their lines, caught the Allied forces by surprise. Due to troop positioning, the Americans bore the brunt of the attack, incurring 100,000 deaths, the highest number of casualties of any battle during the war. However, after a month of grueling fighting in the bitter cold, a lack of fuel and a masterful American military strategy resulted in an Allied victory that sealed Germany's fate.

18) **In the last sentence, the word "grueling" MOST nearly means**

    A.   exhausting.

    B.   secretive.

    C.   costly.

    D.   intermittent.

    E.   ineffective.

The Bastille, Paris's famous historic prison, was originally built in 1370 as a fortification, called a **bastide** in Old French, to protect the city from English invasion during the Hundred Years' War. It rose 100 feet into the air, had eight towers, and was surrounded by a moat more than eighty feet wide. In the seventeenth century, the government converted the fortress into an elite prison for upper-class felons, political disruptors, and spies. Residents of the Bastille arrived by direct order of the king and usually were left there to languish without a trial.

19) **In the first sentence, the word "fortification" MOST nearly means**

    A.   royal castle.

    B.   national symbol.

    C.   seat of government.

    D.   defensive structure.

    E.   secret retreat.

FIGURATIVE LANGUAGE

A figure of speech is a word or phrase with a meaning separate from its literal meaning. Figurative language suggests meaning by pointing to something else. When Shakespeare says, "All the world's a stage, / And all the men and women merely players," he is speaking of the world as if it were a stage. Since the world is not literally a stage, the reader has to ask how the world is a stage and what Shakespeare is implying about the world.

Figurative language extends the meaning of words by giving readers a new way to view a subject. Thinking of the world as a stage on which people are performing is a new way of thinking about life. After reading Shakespeare's metaphor, people may reflect on how often they play a role or act a part. They may wonder when their behavior is genuine, whether they are too worried about others evaluating their performance, and so on. Figurative language—such as metaphors and similes—generates thought after thought. With just a few words, it engages the reader's imagination and adds emphasis to different aspects of the text's subject.

HELPFUL HINT

Aristotle claimed that "the greatest thing by far is to have a command of metaphor. This alone cannot be imparted by another; it is the mark of genius, for to make good metaphors implies an eye for resemblances." The resemblance between two unlike things enables understanding of the ideas suggested by metaphoric language.

A **metaphor** is a figure of speech that expresses an unfamiliar *topic* in terms of a familiar *vehicle*. The familiar vehicle helps the reader understand an unfamiliar topic. Readers reflect on the similarities between the topic and the vehicle and form a new idea about the topic. For example, if a person refers to an issue as "the elephant in the room," the topic is the issue, and "the elephant in the room" is the vehicle. In this example, the vehicle shows that the issue is undeniable or overwhelming.

In **personification**, an object is anthropomorphized—receives a human attribute. In the sentence "The earth swallowed him whole," "earth" is personified: it carries out a human action. Personification may also represent an abstract quality. For instance, a timid individual may be the "personification of cowardice."

A **simile** directly points to similarities between two things. The author uses a familiar vehicle to express an idea about the topic. For example, in his poem "The Rime of the Ancient Mariner," Samuel Taylor Coleridge describes his ship as "Idle as a painted ship upon a painted ocean." Since most readers have seen a painting of a ship, Coleridge uses this knowledge to convey that the ship was completely motionless. Like a simile, an **analogy** is a correspondence between two things; it shows a partial similarity.

SAMPLE QUESTION

Alfie closed his eyes and took several deep breaths. He was trying to ignore the sounds of the crowd, but even he had to admit that it was hard not to notice the tension in the stadium. He could feel 50,000 sets of eyes burning through his skin—this crowd expected perfection from him. He took another breath and opened his eyes, setting his sights on the soccer ball resting peacefully in the grass. One shot, just one last shot, between his team and the championship. He didn't look up at the goalie, who was jumping nervously on the goal line just a few yards away. Afterward, he would swear he didn't remember anything between the referee's whistle and the thunderous roar of the crowd.

20) Which sentence BEST describes the meaning of the phrase "He could feel 50,000 sets of eyes burning through his skin"?

    A. The 50,000 people in the stadium were trying to hurt Alfie.

    B. Alfie felt uncomfortable and exposed in front of so many people.

    C. Alfie felt immense pressure from the 50,000 people watching him.

    D. The people in the stadium are warning Alfie that the field is on fire.

    E. The crowd was angry at Alfie.

COMPARING PASSAGES

Some of the questions in the Praxis Reading exam ask test takers to compare texts with similar themes or topics. Test takers will have to identify the similarities and differences in main ideas, styles, supporting details, and text structures. Previewing the questions and noting similarities and differences in texts while reading will be helpful.

The following passages discuss cicadas, a common insect in the United States. Readers should keep in mind the following questions:

▶   What central idea about cicadas is being expressed in the passages?

▶   How does the tone of Passage A differ from that of Passage B?

SAMPLE QUESTIONS

Passage A
Cicadas are familiar to many Americans due to their buzzing, clicking song. In the eastern part of the United States, during the summer the air echoes with the humming of the cicada, an oval-shaped insect that can reach up to 2.5 inches in length. Cicadas are harmless: they do not sting or bite humans. They emerge from the ground in the summer to mate. Cicadas live underground as juveniles, or nymphs, and shed their skin, or exoskeletons, to take on their adult form. Cicadas are found in Texas, the southeastern United States, the mid-Atlantic, and range up through New York State and southern New England. They also inhabit the Midwest.

Passage B
The sounds of summer in the eastern United States feature the lazy buzzing of the cicada. Did you know that there are actually two kinds of cicadas? Some breeds emerge every year to hum away through the hot summer days. Others spend thirteen or even seventeen years underground as babies, or nymphs, only coming out into the light after all that time to mate and die! Cicadas may look a little scary, but don't worry: they are not a threat to humans. Even though they can get quite large for insects, growing to up to 2.5 inches, they eat twigs and liquid from plants. Adult cicadas do not eat at all. They only live for a short time to mate.

21) **What argument do both sources share about cicadas?**

   A.   Cicadas live throughout the United States.

   B.   The sound of cicadas is familiar to Americans in the eastern United States.

   C.   Cicadas are dangerous insects because they are poisonous.

   D.   American crops are plagued by cicadas every summer.

   E.   The western states are home to cicadas that emerge every seventeen years.

22) **What is the main difference between the passages?**

   A.   Passage A discusses the geographic range of cicadas. Passage B discusses what they eat.

   B.   Passage A talks about the cicadas that emerge every seventeen years. Passage B does not.

   C.   Passage A has a more formal tone, while Passage B has a more informal tone.

   D.   Passage A argues that cicadas are important in the environment. Passage B warns of their harm.

   E.   Passage A was written by a scientist. Passage B was written by a student.

ANSWER KEY

1) A. Incorrect. The author lists Custer's family members who died in the battle, but this is not the main idea.

    B. Incorrect. The author states this fact, but it is not the main idea.

    C. Incorrect. The author does not explain why the cavalry was formed.

    D. Incorrect. The author does not describe the relationship between Sitting Bull and Custer.

    E. Correct. The author writes, "the allied tribes…decisively defeated their US foes."

2) A. Incorrect. The author describes Molaison's memory loss, but this is not the main idea of the passage.

    B. Correct. The author writes, "From this, scientists learned that different types of memory are handled by different parts of the brain."

    C. Incorrect. The author does explain the differences in long-term and short-term memory formation, but not until the end of the passage.

    D. Incorrect. Although the author implies that memories of physical skills are processed differently than memories of events, this is not the main idea of the passage.

    E. Incorrect. The author states that "the hippocampus [is] responsible for *episodic memory*, the short-term recall of events," not all memories related to events.

3) A. Incorrect. This is the last sentence of the passage and summarizes the passage's content.

    B. Correct. This is the first sentence of the passage and introduces the topic: limitations on government provided by the US Constitution.

    C. Incorrect. This is a supporting sentence in the body of the passage. These types of sentences give important details that support the main idea.

    D. Incorrect. This is another supporting sentence with details that support the main idea.

    E. Incorrect. This is another sentence containing supporting details.

4) **A. Correct.** This is the last sentence of the passage and summarizes the passage's content.

    B. Incorrect. This is the first sentence of the passage and introduces the topic: limitations on government provided by the US Constitution.

    C. Incorrect. This is a supporting sentence found in the body of the passage. These types of sentences give important details that support the main idea of the passage.

    D. Incorrect. This is also a supporting sentence with details that support the main idea.

E.   Incorrect. This is another sentence containing supporting details.

5) A.   Incorrect. The author mentions magnetic and gravitational fields on Saturn, not Titan.

    B.   Incorrect. The author writes, "Then it passed through the unexplored region between Saturn itself and its famous rings." The passage does not mention any rings on Titan.

    C.   Correct. The author writes, "First…it recorded data on Titan's curious methane lakes, gathering information about potential seasons on the planet-sized moon."

    D.   Incorrect. The author refers to the rings of Saturn, not of Titan, when stating, "Scientists hope to learn how old the rings are."

    E.   Incorrect. The author writes that *Cassini* "provided scientists with unprecedented information about Saturn's atmosphere," not Titan's.

6) **A.   Correct.** A company that profits from private tutoring might be biased in a study on the effects of private tutoring in schools.

    B.   Incorrect. This type of study would likely strengthen the author's argument by reinforcing the conclusion that private tutoring leads to educational inequality.

    C.   Incorrect. Statements from local teachers would not weaken the author's argument about educational inequality because they are subjective and would not ensure equal opportunity.

    D.   Incorrect. The study is not focused on college success.

    E.   Incorrect. A pricing schedule for private tutors would strengthen the author's argument by highlighting the lack of access for students whose parents could not afford the prices.

7) A.   Incorrect. This answer choice provides fact-based instructions, not an opinion.

    B.   Correct. The writer uses the first person, showing his or her opinion, to recommend a French press as the best way to brew coffee.

    C.   Incorrect. This answer choice provides fact-based information about the process of brewing coffee.

    D.   Incorrect. This answer choice provides fact-based instructions, not an opinion.

    E.   Incorrect. This answer choice provides fact-based instructions about the process of brewing coffee.

8) A.   Incorrect. There is not enough detailed evidence to infer the Confederate reaction to the march.

    B.   Correct. The author describes the level of destruction in detail, suggesting it had a significant negative impact on the Confederacy.

C. Incorrect. The author does not describe any response to the march.

D. Incorrect. The author writes, "Sherman estimated his troops inflicted $100 million in damages."

E. Incorrect. The author does not address the importance of Savannah to the Confederacy.

9) A. Incorrect. The author provides no evidence that invasive species typically help native species.

B. Incorrect. The author writes that the quagga mussels, an invasive species, harmed native species.

C. Incorrect. The author implies that quagga mussels are thriving.

D. **Correct.** The author writes that "the reason for the cisco's reemergence is even more unlikely. The cisco have an invasive species, quagga mussels, to thank for their return."

E. Incorrect. The author describes how quagga mussels are taking nutrients from other invasive species but gives no evidence that this is common.

10) A. Incorrect. The author does not address the impact of the gun on troops.

B. Incorrect. The author does not offer an opinion on the use of the Gatling gun.

C. **Correct.** The author explains why the gun was created, how it functions, and how it was first used.

D. Incorrect. The author does not describe the impact of the Gatling gun on combat fatalities.

E. Incorrect. The author does not address the modern machine gun at all.

11) A. **Correct.** The passage explains how a baby's senses develop and allow him or her to interact with the world.

B. Incorrect. The passage does not tell a story.

C. Incorrect. The passage is not intended to change the reader's opinions or behaviors.

D. Incorrect. The passage provides facts, not descriptions.

E. Incorrect. The passage relies on facts, not emotional or logical arguments.

12) A. Incorrect. The author does describe the development of certain senses in babies in chronological order.

B. Incorrect. The author does not focus on a cause-effect relationship.

C. Incorrect. The author does not introduce a problem and provide a solution.

D. **Correct.** The author draws a contrast between the way vision and the other senses develop in babies.

E. Incorrect. The author provides some description, but this is not the main structure of the text.

13) A.   Incorrect. The author mentions these qualities but does not give an opinion on them.

     B.   **Correct.** The purpose of the passage is to explain what an idealist believes in. The author does not offer any opinions or try to persuade readers about the importance of certain values.

     C.   Incorrect. The author states that social and political discourse are "permeated with idealism" but does not suggest that this is destructive or wrong.

     D.   Incorrect. The author provides the reader with information but does not seek to change the reader's opinions or behaviors.

     E.   Incorrect. The author provides information about how idealists view the truth but does not necessarily intend for readers to question it.

14) A.   Incorrect. Though the author mentions some details of his personal life, most of his letter is concerned with work-related matters.

     B.   Incorrect. Though the author is primarily concerned with work-related matters, he includes personal details and friendly language.

     C.   **Correct.** The author and Alan have a friendly relationship, as evidenced by the author's casual tone and his offer to bring Alan a gift from his vacation.

     D.   Incorrect. The author's tone is casual, and he includes details that suggest he is not concerned or stressed about how things will go in his absence.

     E.   Incorrect. Though the author shares some personal details in his letter, he does not share very many, and he is more focused on work-related matters.

15) A.   Incorrect. The author asks Alan if he wants any special treats, but since this is the last sentence of the letter, it cannot be the main purpose.

     B.   Incorrect. The author's tone is not boastful. He discusses professional matters and offers to bring Alan a gift, showing consideration.

     C.   **Correct.** The author is writing to tell Alan that he will be out of the office. The details about his trip and the meeting support this idea.

     D.   Incorrect. The author mentions the meeting but not how Alan should prepare.

     E.   Incorrect. The author mentions Joanie but does not suggest that he is introducing them for the first time.

16) **A.**   **Correct.** The word "incentivize" is defined immediately with the synonym "motivate," or to encourage.

17) **C.**   **Correct.** The reader can use context clues to determine that the pressure to perform is making the student anxious.

18) **A.**   **Correct.** The context implies that the fighting was intense and tiring.

19) **D. Correct.** The author writes that the Bastille was originally built "to protect the city from English invasion during the Hundred Years' War."

20) A. Incorrect. Because the crowd "expected perfection from" Alfie, the reader can assume they are on his side. There is no indication that they want to hurt him.

   B. Incorrect. The author implies that Alfie is nervous about taking the shot but not that he feels uncomfortable or exposed.

   C. Correct. The metaphor implies that Alfie felt pressure from the people watching him to perform well. There is no indication that he is threatened physically.

   D. Incorrect. The author gives no indication that Alfie is in actual physical danger.

   E. Incorrect. The author gives no indication that the crowd is angry with Alfie, only that they "expected perfection from him."

21) A. Incorrect. Both passages state that cicadas inhabit the eastern United States. Passage A is more specific, stating, "Cicadas are found in Texas, the southeastern United States, the mid-Atlantic, and range up through New York State and southern New England. They also inhabit the Midwest."

   B. Correct. Both passages mention the song of cicadas throughout the eastern United States. Passage A states, "In the eastern part of the United States, during the summer the air echoes with the humming of the cicada." According to Passage B, "The sounds of summer in the eastern United States feature the lazy buzzing of the cicada."

   C. Incorrect. Both passages specifically state that cicadas are not dangerous to humans.

   D. Incorrect. Passage A mentions that cicadas are "harmless" but not what they eat. Passage B says that cicadas "eat twigs and liquid from plants" and that "[a]dult cicadas do not eat at all."

   E. Incorrect. Both passages point out that cicadas inhabit the eastern states, not the western ones.

22) A. Incorrect. Both passages discuss where cicadas live.

   B. Incorrect. The reverse is true.

   C. Correct. Passage A has a more formal tone, and Passage B uses a more informal tone with contractions and direct address: "Did you know that there are actually two kinds of cicadas?... Cicadas may look a little scary, but don't worry…"

   D. Incorrect. Neither passage discusses the impact of cicadas on the environment.

   E. Incorrect. The authors are not identified. While Passage B has a less formal tone than Passage A, that does not mean that Passage A was written by a scientist. There is no way to be sure.

2

Language and Research Skills

PARTS OF SPEECH

The **parts of speech** are the building blocks of sentences, paragraphs, and entire texts. There are eight parts of speech: nouns, pronouns, verbs, adverbs, adjectives, conjunctions, prepositions, and interjections. Each plays a unique role in a sentence.

The exam tests the reader's ability to identify errors in sentences. Readers will need a basic knowledge of the parts of speech to answer these questions correctly.

NOUNS AND PRONOUNS

Nouns give names to people, places, things, and ideas. Nouns are usually the subject or object in a sentence.

There are several types of nouns: common nouns ("chair," "car," "house"), proper nouns ("Julie," "David"), abstract nouns ("love," "intelligence," "sadness"), concrete nouns ("window," "bread," "person"), compound nouns ("brother-in-law," "roller coaster"), non-countable nouns ("money," "water"), countable nouns ("dollars," "cubes"), and verbal nouns ("writing," "diving").

> **HELPFUL HINT**
>
> The subject performs the action of a sentence, while the object has the action performed on it.

In the following sentence, there are three nouns: "family," "cabin," and "lake":

The <u>family</u> visited the <u>cabin</u> by the <u>lake</u>.

Writers use **pronouns** to replace nouns in a sentence or paragraph to avoid repetition. The noun that a pronoun replaces is called its **antecedent**.

Pronouns fall into several categories. Some of the basic types of pronouns are listed in Table 2.1.

Table 2.1. Pronouns

Pronoun Type	Purpose	Example
Personal pronouns	act as subjects or objects in a sentence	<u>She</u> received a letter; <u>I</u> gave the letter to <u>her</u>.
Possessive pronouns	indicate possession	<u>My</u> coat is red; <u>our</u> car is blue.
Reflexive pronouns	intensify or reflect back on a noun	I <u>myself</u> made the dessert. I made the dessert <u>myself</u>.

Personal, possessive, and reflexive pronouns must agree with the noun they replace in gender (male, female, or neutral), number (singular or plural), and person.

Person refers to the point of view. First person is the point of view of the speaker ("I," "me"), second person is the person being addressed ("you"), and third person refers to a person outside the sentence ("he," "she," "they").

Table 2.2. Personal, Possessive, and Reflexive Pronouns

Case	First Person		Second Person		Third Person	
	singular	*plural*	*singular*	*plural*	*singular*	*plural*
Subject	I	we	you	you (all)	he, she, it	they
Object	me	us	you	you (all)	him, her, it	them
Possessive	my	our	your	your	his, her, its	their
Reflexive	myself	ourselves	yourself	yourselves	himself, herself, itself	themselves

Table 2.3. Indefinite Pronouns

Singular		Plural	Singular or Plural
each	everybody	both	some
either	nobody	few	any
neither	somebody	several	none
one	anybody	many	all
everyone	everything		most
no one	nothing		more
someone	something		
anyone	anything		
	another		

Indefinite pronouns replace nouns to avoid unnecessary repetition:

> My friend asked me to choose between two dresses,
> but I like <u>both</u>.

Indefinite pronouns can be singular or plural (and some can act as both, depending on the context). If the indefinite pronoun is the subject of the sentence, it is important to know whether that pronoun is singular or plural so the verb can agree with the pronoun in number.

SAMPLE QUESTIONS

1) **Which pronoun correctly completes the sentence?**

   My wife taught me to drive stick shift so ___ could use her car while mine was in the shop.

   A.   you

   B.   I

   C.   my

   D.   his

   E.   us

2) **Which pronoun correctly completes the sentence?**

   _____ believes that going to a party the night before your certification exam is a bad idea.

   A.   Everybody

   B.   Something

   C.   Several

   D.   Few

   E.   Many

VERBS

Verbs express action ("run," "jump," "play") or state of being ("is," "seems"). Verbs can stand alone, or they can be accompanied by **helping verbs**, which are used to indicate tense.

Verb tense indicates the time of the action. The action may have occurred in the past, may be occurring in the present, or might occur in the future. The action may also have been simple (occurring once) or continuous (ongoing). The perfect and perfect continuous tenses describe when actions occur in relation to other actions.

> **HELPFUL HINT**
>
> Helping verbs include: is, am, are, was, were; be, being, been; has, had, have; do, does, did; should, would, could; will

Table 2.4. Verb Tenses

Tense	Past	Present	Future
Simple	I <u>answered</u> the question.	I <u>answer</u> your questions in class.	I <u>will answer</u> your question.
Continuous	I <u>was answering</u> your question when you interrupted me.	I <u>am answering</u> your question; please listen.	I <u>will be answering</u> your question after the lecture.
Perfect	I <u>had answered</u> all questions before class ended.	I <u>have answered</u> the questions already.	I <u>will have answered</u> every question before the class is over.
Perfect continuous	I <u>had been answering</u> questions when the students started leaving.	I <u>have been answering</u> questions for thirty minutes and am getting tired.	I <u>will have been answering</u> students' questions for twenty years by the time I retire.

Changing the spelling of a verb and/or adding helping verbs is called **conjugation**. In addition to tense, verbs are conjugated to indicate *person* (first, second, and third) and *number* (singular or plural).

The conjugation of the verb must agree with the subject of the sentence. A verb that has not been conjugated is called an infinitive and begins with "to" ("to swim," "to be").

Table 2.5. Verb Conjugation (Present Tense)

Person	Singular	Plural
First person	I answer	we answer
Second person	you answer	you (all) answer
Third person	he/she/it answers	they answer

HELPFUL HINT

A noun that receives the direct object is the indirect object: "The pitcher will throw <u>Antoine</u> the ball."

Finally, verbs can be classified by whether they take a **direct object**, a noun that receives the action of the verb. **Transitive verbs** require a direct object. In the sentence below, the transitive verb "throw" has a direct object (the ball):

The pitcher will throw <u>the ball</u>.

Intransitive verbs do not require a direct object. Verbs like "run," "jump," and "go" make sense without any object:

He will run.

> She jumped.

Many sets of similar verbs include one transitive and one intransitive verb, which can cause confusion. Some troublesome verb combinations include lie/lay, rise/raise, and sit/set. The exam may test on these. Some commonly confused intransitive and transitive verbs are listed in the table below.

Table 2.6. Intransitive and Transitive Verbs	
Intransitive Verbs	**Transitive Verbs**
lie: to recline	lay: to put (lay <u>something</u>)
rise: to go or get up	raise: to lift (raise <u>something</u>)
sit: to be seated	set: to put (set <u>something</u>)
Hint: These intransitive verbs have *i* as the second letter. "Intransitive" begins with *i*.	Hint: The word "transitive" begins with a *t*, and it *TAKES* an object.

SAMPLE QUESTIONS

3) **Choose the correctly conjugated verb to complete the sentence.**

   By this time tomorrow, I _____ my exam.
   - A. finish
   - B. will finish
   - C. will have finished
   - D. had finished
   - E. have been finishing

4) **Which sentence contains an error?**
   - A. Please sit the plate down on the table.
   - B. She lay the towel on the sand at the beach.
   - C. Students should raise their hands if they have a question.
   - D. Every morning, the sun rises.
   - E. On Sundays, I lie on the couch and watch TV if I'm not busy.

ADJECTIVES AND ADVERBS

Adjectives modify, or describe, nouns and pronouns. In English, adjectives are usually placed before the word being modified, although they can also come after a linking verb such as "is" or "smells":

> The <u>beautiful</u> <u>blue</u> <u>jade</u> necklace will go perfectly with my dress.

> I think that lasagna smells <u>delicious</u>.

The suffixes –*er* and –*est* are used to modify adjectives in a comparison. The suffix –*er* is used when comparing two things, and the suffix –*est* is used when comparing more than two:

> Anne is <u>taller</u> than Steve, but Steve is <u>more coordinated</u>.

> Of the five brothers, Jordan is the <u>funniest</u>, and Alex is the <u>most intelligent</u>.

Adjectives longer than two syllables are compared using "more" (for two things) or "most" (for three or more things):

> **Incorrect**: Of my <u>two</u> friends, Clara is <u>the smartest</u>.

> **Correct**: Of my <u>two</u> friends, Clara is <u>smarter</u>.

"More" and "most" should not be used with –*er* and –*est* endings:

> **Incorrect**: My <u>most warmest</u> sweater is made of wool.

> **Correct**: My <u>warmest</u> sweater is made of wool.

Adverbs, which are often formed by adding the suffix –*ly*, modify any word (or set of words) that is not a noun or pronoun:

> He quickly ran to the house next door. ("Quickly" modifies the verb "ran.")

> Her very effective speech earned her a promotion. ("Very" modifies the adjective "effective.")

HELPFUL HINT

Adverbs typically answer the questions Where? When? Why? How? How often? To what extent? Under what conditions?

SAMPLE QUESTION

5)   **Which of the following sentences contains an adjective error?**
   A.   The new red car was faster than the old blue car.
   B.   Reggie's apartment is in the tallest building on the block.
   C.   The slice of cake was tastier than the brownie.
   D.   Of the four speeches, Jerry's was the most long.
   E.   Aubrey is my favorite colleague.

CONJUNCTIONS

Conjunctions join words into phrases, clauses, and sentences. There are three main types of conjunctions: coordinating, correlative, and subordinating.

Coordinating conjunctions join together two independent clauses (i.e., two complete thoughts). These include "for," "and," "nor," "but," "or," "yet," "so" (the acronym FANBOYS can help you remember these words). Note that some of these can also be used to join items in a series:

> I will order lunch, <u>but</u> you need to go pick it up.

> Make sure to get sandwiches, chips, <u>and</u> sodas.

Correlative conjunctions (whether/or, either/or, neither/nor, both/and, not only/but also) work together to join items:

> <u>Both</u> the teacher <u>and</u> the students needed a break after the lecture.

When connecting two subjects with correlative conjunctions, the second one must agree with the verb that follows:

> **Incorrect**: I will <u>neither</u> mow the grass <u>nor</u> do I want to pull weeds today.

> **Correct**: I will <u>neither</u> mow the grass <u>nor</u> pull the weeds today.

Subordinating conjunctions join dependent clauses (thoughts that cannot stand alone as sentences) to the related independent clause. They usually describe a relationship between the two parts of the sentence, such as cause-effect or order. They can appear at the beginning or in the middle of a sentence:

HELPFUL HINT

The exam does not test the names of the different conjunctions, but it will test on sentence errors caused by misused conjunctions.

> We treat ourselves during football season to several orders <u>because</u> we love pizza.

> <u>Because</u> we love pizza, we treat ourselves during football season to several orders.

6)   **Which sentence contains an error?**
   A.   I don't know whether I'll be available tomorrow.
   B.   Although she was cold, she hesitated before turning off the air-conditioning.
   C.   Neither my mother nor my father has been to Canada.
   D.   Because I was hungry and didn't bring any lunch.
   E.   Everyone I know has flood insurance because it rains so much here.

PREPOSITIONS

Prepositions set up relationships in time ("<u>after</u> the party") or space ("<u>under</u> the cushions") in a sentence. A preposition will always function as part of a prepositional phrase, which includes the preposition and the object of the preposition:

<blockquote>I ran <u>over the river</u> and <u>through the woods</u>.</blockquote>

In the above example, the prepositions are "over" and "through." The prepositional phrases are "over the river" and "through the woods."

Table 2.7. Common Prepositions

Prepositions	Compound Prepositions
along, among, around, at, before, behind, below, beneath, beside, besides, between, beyond, by, despite, down, during, except, for, from, in, into, near, of, off, on, onto, out, outside, over, past, since, through, till, to, toward, under, underneath, until, up, upon, with, within, without	according to, as of, as well as, aside from, because of, by means of, in addition to, in front of, in place of, in respect to, in spite of, instead of, on account of, out of, prior to, with regard to

Interjections, words like "hey" or "wow" are parts of speech. They have no grammatical attachment to the sentence other than to add expressions of emotion. They may be punctuated with commas or exclamation points and may appear anywhere in a sentence: "<u>Ouch</u>! He stepped on my toe."

7)   **Which preposition correctly completes this sentence?**
   I threw the ball _____ my friend.
   A.   among
   B.   since
   C.   during
   D.   in
   E.   to

CONSTRUCTING SENTENCES

In English, words are used to build phrases and clauses. These are then combined to create sentences. Phrases and clauses are made up of a subject, a predicate, or both.

The **subject** is what the sentence is about. It is usually a noun that performs the main action of the sentence, and it may be accompanied by modifiers. The **predicate** describes what the subject is doing or being. It contains the verb(s) and any modifiers or objects that accompany it.

On the exam, you will need to identify errors in sentence structure, including sentence fragments, poorly constructed sentences, run-on sentences, dangling modifiers, and more.

PHRASES

A **phrase** is a group of words that communicates a partial idea and lacks either a subject or a predicate. Phrases are categorized based on the main word in the phrase. A **prepositional phrase** (discussed above) begins with a preposition and ends with an object of the preposition:

> The dog is hiding under the porch.

A **verb phrase** is composed of the main verb and its helping verbs:

> The chef would have created another soufflé,
> but the staff protested.

A **noun phrase** consists of a noun and its modifiers:

> The big, red barn rests beside the vacant chicken house.

When looking for grammatical errors on the exam, test takers should be alert for questions that include phrases masquerading as sentences. A long, complicated phrase can be confused for a complete sentence ("The enthusiastic new student in the class with the blue sweatshirt and the blonde hair"). Remember: a sentence always has a subject and a predicate; a phrase will have only one of those.

SAMPLE QUESTION

8) **Which of the following contains an error?**

    A.   Ten cats in a row.

    B.   My teacher was late today.

    C.   All applicants participate.

    D.   Clouds fill the sky.

    E.   Ice cream is my favorite dessert.

CLAUSES

Clauses contain both a subject and a predicate. They can be either independent or dependent. An **independent** (or main) **clause** can stand alone as its own sentence:

> The dog ate her homework.

Dependent (or subordinate) **clauses** cannot stand alone as their own sentences. They start with a subordinating conjunction, relative pronoun, or relative adjective, which will make them sound incomplete:

> Because the dog ate her homework

Table 2.8. Words That Begin Dependent Clauses

Subordinating Conjunctions	Pronouns and Adjectives
after, although, as, because, before, even if, even though, if, in order that, once, provided, since, so, so that, than, that, though, unless, until, when, whenever, where, whereas, wherever, whether, while	how, that, when, where, which, who, whoever, whom, whomever, whose, why

SAMPLE QUESTION

9) **Which of the following contains an error?**

    A. I watch TV while I knit.

    B. She called me before she left.

    C. You ate more than he did.

    D. Whenever I visit her.

    E. I drove because I was late.

COMPOSING A SENTENCE

Every sentence needs at least one independent clause. For example, the following independent clause is a complete sentence:

> The cat jumped.

There is a subject, "cat," and a verb, "jumped."

Other elements, like phrases and clauses, can be added:

> The cat jumped onto the porch.

In the above sentence, the subject is "The cat," the verb is "jumped," and a prepositional phrase has been added for context: "onto the porch."

Additional clauses can be added. As sentences become more complicated, writers may need to use punctuation or conjunctions (see "Conjunctions" and "Punctuation" in this chapter for more information):

> The cat jumped onto the porch; it then walked into the house.

> The cat jumped onto the porch, and it looked in the window.

In the above sentences, an independent clause has been joined to the original sentence. In the first sentence, the independent clause "it then walked into the house" is connected with a semicolon. In the second sentence, the independent clause "it looked in the window" is connected with the coordinating conjunction "and" and a comma.

To link a dependent clause, commas may or may not be required, depending on context. Commas are discussed in more detail below (see "Punctuation"):

> The cat jumped onto the porch because it wanted to
> get out of the rain.

The clause "because it wanted to get out of the rain" cannot stand on its own. It must be connected to an independent clause.

Questions on the exam may ask about errors in sentence structure. For example, you may be asked to identify the error in a compound sentence in which the independent clauses are connected incorrectly.

SAMPLE QUESTION

10) Which of the following would be the BEST way to write the underlined portion of the sentence?

While these incidents sometimes end in funny or heartwarming <u>stories at other times they</u> end in fear and destruction.

A. stories, at

B. stories; at

C. stories: at

D. stories—at

E. stories. At

PUNCTUATION

The main **punctuation marks** are periods, question marks, exclamation marks, colons, semicolons, commas, quotation marks, and apostrophes.

There are three terminal punctuation marks used to end sentences.

▶ The **period** ends declarative (statement) and imperative (command) sentences.

▶ The **question mark** ends interrogative sentences.
▶ **Exclamation marks** indicate that the writer or speaker is exhibiting intense emotion or energy.

> Sarah and I are attending a concert.

> How many people are attending the concert?

> What a great show that was!

The **colon** and the **semicolon**, though often confused, have a unique set of rules about their respective uses. While both punctuation marks are used to join clauses, the construction of the clauses and the relationship between them is different.

The **semicolon** is used to show a general relationship between two independent clauses (IC; IC):

> The disgruntled customer tapped angrily on the counter; she had to wait nearly ten minutes to speak to the manager.

Coordinating conjunctions (*FANBOYS*, discussed on page 39) cannot be used with semicolons. However, conjunctive adverbs can be used following a semicolon:

> She may not have to take the course this year; however, she will eventually have to sign up for that specific course.

The **colon**, somewhat less limited than the semicolon in its usage, is used to introduce a list, a definition, or a clarification. The clause preceding the colon must be an independent clause, but the clause that follows does not have to be:

> **Incorrect**: The buffet offers three choices that include: ham, turkey, or roast.

> **Correct**: The buffet offers three choices: ham, turkey, or roast.

> **Correct**: The buffet offers three choices that include the following: ham, turkey, or roast.

Note that neither the semicolon nor the colon should be used to set off an introductory phrase from the rest of the sentence:

> **Incorrect**: After the trip to the raceway; we realized that we should have brought earplugs.

> **Incorrect**: After the trip to the raceway: we realized that we should have brought earplugs.

> **Correct**: After the trip to the raceway, we realized that we should have brought earplugs.

The **comma** is a complicated type of punctuation that can serve many different purposes in a sentence. Comma placement is often an issue of style, not mechanics, meaning there may not be only one correct way to write the sentence. There are, however, a few important hard-and-fast comma rules.

1. Commas should be used to separate two independent clauses along with a coordinating conjunction:

   > Khalid ordered the steak, but Bruce preferred the ham.

2. Commas should be used to separate coordinate adjectives (two different adjectives that describe the same noun):

   > The shiny, regal horse ran majestically through the wide, open field.

3. Commas should be used to separate items in a series. The comma before the conjunction is called the Oxford, or serial, comma. (It is optional and will not appear on the exam.)

   > The list of groceries included cream, coffee, donuts, and tea.

4. Commas should be used to separate introductory words, phrases, and clauses from the rest of the sentence:

   > Slowly, Nathan became aware of his surroundings after the concussion.

   > Within an hour, the authorities will descend on the home.

   > After Alice swam the channel, nothing intimidated her.

5. Commas should be used to set off appositive phrases: descriptors that are not needed for the sentence to make sense grammatically:

   > Estelle, our newly elected chairperson, will be in attendance.

   > Ida, my neighbor, watched the children for me last week.

6. Commas should be used to set off titles of famous individuals:

   > Charles, Prince of Wales, visited Canada several times in the last ten years.

7. Commas should be used to set off the day and month of a date:

   > I was born on February 16, 1958, in Minnesota.

8. Commas should be used in numbers of more than four digits:

   > We expect 25,000 visitors to the new museum.

Quotation marks are used for many purposes. They are used to enclose direct quotations in a sentence. Terminal punctuation that is part of the quotation goes inside the marks, and terminal punctuation that is part of the larger sentence goes outside:

> She asked him menacingly, "Where is my peanut butter?"

> What is the original meaning of the phrase "king of the hill"?

In American English, commas are used to set quotations apart from the surrounding text and are placed inside the marks:

> "Although I find him tolerable," Arianna wrote, "I would never want him as a roommate."

Additionally, quotation marks enclose titles of short, or relatively short, literary works such as short stories, chapters, and poems (titles of longer works, like novels and anthologies, are italicized):

> For English class, we read "The Raven" by Edgar Allan Poe.

Writers also use quotation marks to set off words used in a special sense or for a nonliterary purpose:

> The shady dealings of his Ponzi scheme earned him the ironic name "Honest Abe."

Apostrophes (sometimes referred to as single quotation marks) have a number of different uses:

▶ show possession
▶ replace missing letters, numerals, and signs
▶ form plurals of letters, numerals, and signs in certain instances

1. To signify possession by a singular noun not ending in *s*, add *'s*:

> boy → boy's

2. To signify possession by a singular noun ending in *s*, add *'s*:

> class → class's

3. To signify possession by an indefinite pronoun not ending in *s*, add *'s*:

> someone → someone's

4. To signify possession by a plural noun not ending in *s*, add *'s*:

> children → children's

5. To signify possession by a plural noun ending in *s*, add only the apostrophe:

> boys → boys'

6. To signify possession by singular, compound words and phrases, add *'s* to the last word in the phrase:

    everybody else → everybody else's

7. To signify joint possession, add *'s* only to the last noun:

    John and Mary's house

8. To signify individual possession, add *'s* to each noun:

    John's and Mary's houses

9. To signify missing letters in a contraction, place the apostrophe where the letters are missing:

    do not → don't

10. To signify missing numerals, place the apostrophe where the numerals are missing:

    1989 → '89

11. There are differing schools of thought regarding the pluralization of numerals and dates, but writers should use one style consistently within the document:

    1990's/1990s; A's/As

SAMPLE QUESTIONS

11) **Which of the following is the correct version of the underlined portion of the sentence below?**

    Fred's brother wanted the following items for <u>Christmas a</u> red car, a condo, and a puppy.

    A. Christmas; a
    B. Christmas, a
    C. Christmas. A
    D. Christmas: a
    E. Christmas' a

12) **Which of the following sentences contains a comma usage error?**

    A. On her way home she stopped to pick up groceries, pay her electric bill, and buy some flowers.
    B. I used to drink coffee every morning but my office took away the coffee machine.
    C. Elizabeth will order the cake for the party after she orders the hats.
    D. My cousin, who lives in Indiana, is coming to visit this weekend.
    E. Before you go to the store you need to make a list.

Capitalization

Capitalization questions will ask about errors in capitalization within a phrase or sentence. Below are the most important rules for capitalization.

The first word of a sentence is always capitalized:

> We will be having dinner at a new restaurant tonight.

The first letter of a proper noun is always capitalized:

> We're going to Chicago on Wednesday.

Titles are capitalized if they precede the name they modify:

> Joe Biden, the vice president, met with President Obama.

Months are capitalized, but not the names of the seasons:

> Snow fell in March even though winter was over.

The names of major holidays should be capitalized. The word "day" is only capitalized if it is part of the holiday's name:

> We always go to a parade on Memorial Day, but Christmas day
> we stay home.

The names of specific places should always be capitalized. General location terms are not capitalized:

> We're going to San Francisco next weekend so I can
> see the ocean.

Titles for relatives should be capitalized when they precede a name, but not when they stand alone:

> Fred, my uncle, will make fried chicken, and Aunt Betty is going
> to make spaghetti.

SAMPLE QUESTION

13) **Which of the following sentences contains a capitalization error?**

    A.   My two brothers are going to New Orleans for Mardi Gras.

    B.   On Friday we voted to elect a new class president.

    C.   Janet wants to go to Mexico this Spring.

    D.   Peter complimented the chef on his cooking.

    E.   The prime minister will meet with the president on Tuesday.

AVOIDING COMMON USAGE ERRORS

Some of the most common grammatical errors are those involving agreement between subjects and verbs, and between nouns and pronouns. While it is impossible to cover all possible errors, the lists below include the most common agreement rules to look for on the test.

ERRORS IN SUBJECT–VERB AGREEMENT

Test takers will be asked to find errors in subject-verb agreement on the exam. To prepare for these questions, practice identifying the subject and the verb in a sentence and review the rules for subject-verb agreement.

1. Single subjects agree with single verbs; plural subjects agree with plural verbs:

    The girl walks her dog.

    The girls walk their dogs.

2. Compound subjects joined by "and" typically take a plural verb unless considered one item:

    Correctness and precision are required for all good writing.

    Macaroni and cheese makes a great snack for children.

3. Compound subjects joined by "or" or "nor" agree with the nearer or nearest subject:

    Neither I nor my friends are looking forward to our final exams.

    Neither my friends nor I am looking forward to our final exams.

4. For sentences with inverted word order, the verb will agree with the subject that follows it:

    Where are Bob and his friends going?

    Where is Bob going?

5. All single, indefinite pronouns agree with single verbs:

    Neither of the students is happy about the play.

    Each of the many cars is on the grass.

    Every one of the administrators speaks highly of Trevor.

6. All plural, indefinite pronouns agree with plural verbs:

    Several of the students are happy about the play.

> Both of the cars are on the grass.

> Many of the administrators speak highly of Trevor.

7. Collective nouns agree with singular verbs when the collective acts as one unit. Collective nouns agree with plural verbs when the collective acts as individuals within the group:

> The band plans a party after the final football game.

> The band play their instruments even if it rains.

> The jury announces its decision after sequestration.

> The jury make phone calls during their break time.

8. Nouns that are plural in form but singular in meaning will agree with singular verbs:

> Measles is a painful disease.

> Sixty dollars is too much to pay for that book.

9. Singular verbs come after titles, business names, and words used as terms:

> "Three Little Kittens" is a favorite nursery rhyme for many children.

> General Motors is a major employer for the city.

Ignore words between the subject and the verb to help make conjugation clearer:

> The new library with its many books and rooms fills a long-felt need.

SAMPLE QUESTION

14) **Which sentence does NOT contain an error?**
   A. My sister and my best friend lives in Chicago.
   B. My parents or my brother is going to pick me up from the airport.
   C. Neither of the students refuse to take the exam.
   D. The team were playing a great game until the rain started.
   E. The store, which sells magazines and books, close early on Mondays.

PRONOUN–ANTECEDENT AGREEMENT AND PRONOUN ERRORS

Pronoun errors are commonly tested on the exam. Below are some of the more common pronoun rules that may appear on the test.

1. The antecedent and pronoun must agree in gender and number:

   I baked a cake for my <u>mother</u> because it was <u>her</u> birthday.

2. Antecedents joined by "and" require a plural pronoun:

   The <u>children and their dogs</u> enjoyed <u>their</u> day at the beach.

3. For antecedents joined by "or," the pronoun agrees with the nearest antecedent:

   Either the resident mice <u>or the manager's cat</u> gets <u>itself</u> a meal of good leftovers.

4. The pronoun must agree with the number of the indefinite pronouns:

   <u>Neither</u> student finished <u>her</u> assignment.

   <u>Both</u> of the students finished <u>their</u> assignments.

5. When "each" and "every" precede the antecedent, the pronoun should be singular:

   <u>Each child</u> brings unique qualities to <u>his or her</u> family.

   <u>Every writer</u> is attending <u>his or her</u> assigned lecture.

6. If a pronoun leads to ambiguity, do not use it:

   <u>My mom and my sister</u> went to pick up <u>my sister's</u> new phone. (not "her new phone")

   <u>David and Henry</u> lost <u>David's</u> wallet in the park. (not "his wallet")

SAMPLE QUESTION

15) **Which sentence does NOT contain an error?**
   A. The grandchildren and their cousins enjoyed their day at the beach.
   B. Most of the grass has lost their deep color.
   C. The jury was cheering as their commitment came to a close.
   D. Every boy and girl must learn to behave themselves in school.
   E. Each woman brought their baggage to the counter and asked that it be checked.

MODIFIER ERRORS

Adjectives, adverbs, and **modifying phrases** (groups of words that together modify another word) should be placed as close as possible to the word they modify. Separating words from their modifiers can create incorrect or confusing sentences:

> **Incorrect**: <u>Running through the hall, the bell</u> rang, and the student knew she was late.

> **Correct**: <u>Running through the hall, the student</u> heard the bell ring and knew she was late.

Who is running: the bell or the student? The phrase "running through the hall" should be placed next to "student," the noun it modifies. The modifier error in the incorrect sentence is a **dangling modifier**. The modifier is "dangling" in the sentence separately from what it is modifying. This is a common error tested on the exam.

SAMPLE QUESTION

16) **Which of the following sentences contains a structural error?**

   A.   Adult penguins are black and white, but penguin chicks are gray.

   B.   Being allergic to bananas, smoothies were not Donna's preferred breakfast.

   C.   Each unit is scheduled for periodic maintenance when winter is over.

   D.   Sometimes I lie on the floor and read by the fire, or I sit on the couch and watch TV.

   E.   Hurricanes threaten the eastern United States; earthquakes menace the Pacific coast.

Errors in Sentence Construction

Errors in parallelism occur when items in a series are not put in the same form. For example, if a list contains two nouns and a verb, the sentence should be rewritten so that all three items are the same part of speech. Parallelism should be maintained in words, phrases, and clauses:

> The walls were painted <u>green</u> and <u>gold</u>.

> Her home is <u>up the hill</u> and <u>beyond the trees</u>.

> <u>If we shop on Friday</u> and <u>if we have enough time</u>, we will then visit the aquarium.

Sentence errors fall into three categories: fragments, comma splices (comma fault), and fused sentences (run-on). A **fragment** occurs when a group of words lacks both a subject and verb as needed to construct a complete sentence or thought:

> **Incorrect**: Why am I not going to the mall? Because I do not like shopping.

> **Correct**: Because I do not like shopping, I will not plan to go to the mall.

A **comma splice** (comma fault) occurs when two independent clauses are joined together with only a comma to "splice" them together. To fix a comma splice, add a coordinating conjunction or replace the comma with a semicolon:

> **Incorrect**: My family eats turkey at Thanksgiving, we eat ham at Christmas.

> **Correct**: My family eats turkey at Thanksgiving, and we eat ham at Christmas.

> **Correct**: My family eats turkey at Thanksgiving; we eat ham at Christmas.

Fused (run-on) sentences occur when two independent clauses are joined with no punctuation. Like comma splices, they can be fixed with a comma and conjunction or with a semicolon:

> **Incorrect**: My sister lives nearby she never comes to visit.

> **Correct**: My sister lives nearby, but she never comes to visit.

> **Correct**: My sister lives nearby; she never comes to visit.

SAMPLE QUESTIONS

17) **Which of the following would NOT be an acceptable way to revise and combine the underlined portion of these sentences?**

They receive an <u>annual pension payment. The amount of the pension</u> has been reviewed and changed a number of times.

    A.   annual pension payment, the amount of which

    B.   annual pension payment; the amount of the pension

    C.   annual pension payment; over the years since 1958, the amount of the pension

    D.   annual pension payment, the amount of the pension

    E.   annual pension payment; the amount of each payment

18) **Which of the following contains an error in sentence structure?**

    A.   I asked the teacher when the project was due; she said we had two weeks to finish it.

    B.   I love running, to swim, and also going hiking, but I hate camping.

    C.   Most of my friends enjoy soccer, but I prefer basketball.

    D.   The municipal government stated that there would be no budget increase this year.

    E.   Seagulls, considered a nuisance by residents, populate many local beaches.

19) **Which of the following sentences contains a comma splice?**
    A.   Since she went to the store.
    B.   The football game ended in a tie, the underdog caught up in the fourth quarter.
    C.   If we get rid of the bookcase, we'll have enough room for a couch.
    D.   When the players dropped their gloves, a fight broke out on the ice hockey rink floor.
    E.   The teacher bought balloons, hats, and cupcakes for the party.

WORDINESS AND REDUNDANCY

A sentence may be grammatically correct but still confusing because the writer has repeated words or ideas for no logical reason. In some forms of writing, repetition is purposeful. However, the exam tests a candidate's knowledge of clear and concise writing.

The exam will ask you to clarify wordy sentences or remove redundant phrasing (when several words with similar meanings are used).

Some examples of excessive wordiness and redundancy include:

▸   A memo was sent out <u>concerning the matter of</u> dishes left in the sink. →
     A memo was sent out <u>about</u> dishes left in the sink.

▸   The email was <u>brief and to the point</u>. → The email was <u>terse</u>.

▸   I don't think I'll ever <u>understand or comprehend</u> Italian operas. →
     I don't think I'll ever <u>understand</u> Italian operas.

SAMPLE QUESTION

20) **What is the BEST way to revise this redundant sentence?**

    It was an unexpected surprise to see you this weekend.
    A.   It was a surprise to see you this weekend; we didn't expect it!
    B.   Seeing you this weekend was a surprise!
    C.   We didn't expect to see you this weekend, it was a surprise.
    D.   To be seeing you this weekend, it surprised us.
    E.   We were shocked and surprised to see you this weekend.

COMMONLY CONFUSED WORDS

The exam may feature questions about usage and correct word choice. The list below gives some common sets of words that are often misused. These fall into three general categories:

1.   Homophones: words sound the same but have different meanings (e.g., "insure" and "ensure")

2.   Words with related but distinct meanings (e.g., "amount" and "number")

3. Related words that function as different parts of speech (e.g., "good" and "well")

    ▷   **a, an**: "A" is used before words beginning with consonants or consonant sounds. "An" is used before words beginning with vowels or vowel sounds.

    ▷   **affect, effect**: "Affect" is most often a verb; "effect" is usually a noun. ("The experience <u>affected</u> me significantly" or "The experience had a significant <u>effect</u> on me.")

    ▷   **among, amongst, between**: "Among" is used for a group of more than two people. "Amongst" is archaic and not commonly used in modern writing. "Between" is reserved to distinguish two people, places, things, or groups.

    ▷   **amount, number**: "Amount" is used for non-countable sums; "number" is used with countable nouns. ("She had a large amount of money in her purse, nearly fifty dollars.")

    ▷   **cite, site**: "Cite" is a verb used in documentation to credit an author of a quotation, paraphrase, or summary. "Site" is a location.

    ▷   **elicit, illicit**: "Elicit" means to draw out a response from an audience or a listener. "Illicit" refers to illegal activity.

    ▷   **every day, everyday**: "Every day" is an indefinite adjective modifying a noun—"each day" could be used interchangeably with "every day." "Everyday" is a one-word adjective to describe frequent occurrence. ("Our visit to the Minnesota State Fair is an <u>everyday</u> activity during August.")

    ▷   **fewer, less**: "Fewer" is used with a countable noun; "less" is used with a non-countable noun. ("<u>Fewer</u> parents are experiencing stress since the new teacher was hired" or "Parents are experiencing <u>less</u> stress since the new teacher was hired.")

    ▷   **firstly, secondly**: These words are archaic. Today, "first" and "second" are more commonly used.

    ▷   **good, well**: "Good" is always the adjective; "well" is always the adverb except in cases of health. ("She felt <u>well</u> after the surgery.")

    ▷   **implied, inferred**: "Implied" is something a speaker does; "inferred" is something the listener does after assessing the speaker's message. ("The speaker <u>implied</u> something mysterious, but I <u>inferred</u> the wrong thing.")

    ▷   **irregardless, regardless**: "Irregardless" is nonstandard usage and should be avoided. "Regardless" is the proper usage of the transitional statement.

    ▷   **its, it's**: "Its" is a possessive case pronoun. "It's" is a contraction for "it is."

▷ **moral, morale**: "Moral" is a summative lesson from a story or life event. "Morale" is the emotional attitude of a person or group of people.

▷ **principal, principle**: "Principal" is the leader of a school in the noun usage. "Principal" means *main* in the adjectival usage. "Principle" is also a noun meaning *idea* or *tenet*. ("The <u>principal</u> of the school spoke on the <u>principal</u> meaning of the main <u>principles</u> of the school.")

▷ **quote, quotation**: "Quote" is a verb and should be used as a verb. "Quotation" is the noun and should be used as a noun.

▷ **reason why**: "Reason why" is a redundant expression—use one or the other. ("The <u>reason</u> we left is a secret" or "<u>Why</u> we left is a secret.")

▷ **should of, should have**: "Should of" is improper usage, likely resulting from misunderstood speech—"of" is not a helping verb and therefore cannot complete the verb phrase. "Should have" is the proper usage. ("He <u>should have</u> driven.")

▷ **than, then**: "Than" sets up a comparison of some kind. "Then" indicates a reference to a point in time. ("When I said I liked the hat better <u>than</u> the gloves, my sister laughed; <u>then</u> she bought both for me.")

▷ **their, there, they're**: "Their" is the possessive case of the pronoun "they." "There" is a demonstrative pronoun indicating location, or place. "They're" is a contraction of the words "they are," the third-person plural subject pronoun and third-person plural, present-tense conjugation of the verb "to be." These words are very commonly confused in written English.

▷ **to lie (to recline), to lay (to place)**: "To lie" is the intransitive verb meaning "to recline," so the verb does not take an object. "To lay" is the transitive verb meaning "to place something." ("I <u>lie</u> out in the sun; I <u>lay</u> my towel on the beach.")

▷ **to try and**: "To try and" is sometimes used incorrectly in place of "to try to." ("She should <u>try to</u> succeed daily.")

▷ **unique**: "Unique" is an ultimate superlative. The word "unique" should not be modified technically. ("The experience was <u>unique</u>" not "The experience was <u>very unique</u>.")

▷ **who, whom**: "Who" is a subject-relative pronoun. ("My son, <u>who is</u> a good student, studies hard.") Here, the son is carrying out the action of studying, so the pronoun is a subject pronoun ("who"). "Whom" is the object relative pronoun. ("My son, <u>whom</u> the other students admire, studies hard.") Here, "son" is the object of the other students' admiration, so the pronoun standing in for "him," "whom," is an object pronoun.

▷ **your, you're:** "Your" is the possessive case of the pronoun "you." "You're" is a contraction of the words "you are," the second-person subject pronoun and the second-person singular, present-tense conjugation of the verb "to be." These words are commonly confused in written English.

SAMPLE QUESTION

21) **Identify the error in the following sentence.**

We should have known that the principal reason for the decline in exports was the affect of economic sanctions.

A. should have

B. principal

C. reason

D. affect

E. sanctions

RESEARCH SKILLS

EVALUATING SOURCES

Research is a process of gathering sources containing documented facts that answer specific questions and provide information about an issue. In the twenty-first century, locating sources is easy; however, finding and determining quality sources involves careful evaluation.

It is best to begin by evaluating the credibility of a source's author. A researcher should consider the author's motivation—the purpose or reason he or she had for writing the text. Next, the author's background and expertise should be identified. Although educational credentials are important, firsthand experience offers equally reliable information.

Here are some questions a researcher should be able to answer about a source:

► Is it current or written fairly recently?

► If it is secondary, is it based on primary as well as other, secondary sources?

► Is the author an expert in the area of study? Does he or she include or cite relevant information from other authorities on the topic?

► Are the conclusions based on scientific evidence? How well does the scientifically gathered evidence explain the topic?

► Is the purpose of the source clear? Is there any bias?

► What does the author assume is true?

► Does the author present several viewpoints on issues?

▶   Does the content agree with what other reliable sources on the topic indicate?

When using a website as a source, researchers should evaluate the site's intended audience and if the site has an agenda, such as selling something or promoting a belief system. If the site is educational, researchers should verify whether it was created by authoritative authors and authors who have identified themselves. Grammatically correct content on the site is a helpful indicator. Plus, the site's address should work and be relatively current. (Typing "javascript:alert(document.lastModified)" in the address bar provides a site's most recent modification date.)

SAMPLE QUESTIONS

22) **What legitimizes the claims made in a source?**
   A.   Similar information and conclusions are apparent in other sources.
   B.   The background of the writer is clear.
   C.   The publisher of the source is a respected organization.
   D.   A journalist or an admired writer has written the source.
   E.   The perspective of the author is clear.

23) **A quality source**
   A.   is free of the clutter of citations, quotations, footnotes, and a works-cited page.
   B.   is peer-reviewed by scholars who have credentials in a wide variety of areas, not just the subject of the source article.
   C.   has remained in publication for decades.
   D.   includes accurate, well-documented information.
   E.   provides relevant explanations from one popular perspective.

Types of Sources

The sources a researcher uses depends on his or her purpose. If the purpose is to analyze, interpret, or critique a historical event, a creative work, or a natural phenomenon, the researcher will use a **primary**, or **original**, **source**. Examples of primary sources include:

▶   letters and emails

▶   autobiographies, diaries, and memoirs

▶   firsthand or eyewitness accounts or descriptions of events

▶   interviews, questionnaires, and surveys

▶   speeches and lectures

▶   photographs, drawings, and paintings

▶   news stories written at the time of the event

The written analysis or interpretation of a primary source is considered a **secondary source**. These sources are written by people who do not have firsthand experience of the topic being described. Instead, authors of secondary sources examine primary sources in order to draw conclusions or make generalizations about people, events, and ideas. Examples of secondary sources include:

► literary criticism and interpretation essays

► biographies

► historical criticism

► political analyses

► essays on ethics and social policies

Researchers confronting a problem or question that has not been researched before should analyze the relevant primary documents. In addition, researchers can conduct their own observations, interviews, surveys, or experiments.

If the purpose is to report on, explain, or summarize what is known about a topic, the researcher will use texts written by other researchers or secondary sources. Most primary research studies begin with a review of literature, which summarizes what secondary sources are saying about a topic.

Research on topics of interest usually begins with a critical analysis of existing research. Researchers draw conclusions from secondary sources that deal with their specific topic. Initially, they should consider searching databases. Annotated bibliographies can help locate the most relevant sources for a topic. Webpages created by associations, government agencies, and institutions have a wealth of source material. Although print sources are helpful, most researchers use the internet to find digital versions of print sources. Reports by research agencies are often available, particularly in areas concerning the environment.

If scholarly sources are required—that is, texts written by those who are highly educated in a particular field—Google Scholar and databases like JSTOR, EBSCO, and Gale can be more helpful than a web search. Public libraries are the best places to avoid the cost of subscription-based databases like JSTOR.

SAMPLE QUESTIONS

24) **A secondary source**

    A. summarizes or evaluates an original source or research study.

    B. is written by a person who conducted an original study or wrote an original text.

    C. must be peer reviewed.

    D. is published by the government or a private publisher.

    E. is based on interviews and survey responses.

25) **What kind of source is a political speech?**

A.   a secondary source

B.   an authoritative source

C.   a confusing source

D.   a narrative source

E.   a primary source

RESEARCH STRATEGIES

Research begins with curiosity about a specific topic, then moves from curiosity to a research question. Doing preliminary reading on the topic refines that question and gives the researcher an overview of the topic. A search of **available sources related to the question** is also wise. For example:

- ▸ **Research topic**: Emily Dickinson and feminism
- ▸ **Question**: What feminist ideas did Emily Dickinson express?
- ▸ **Preliminary sources**: Literary criticism on Emily Dickinson, especially feminist interpretations of Dickinson's poetry

Next, the researcher will need to decide which primary sources and critical essays to use. After skim-reading these sources, a preliminary **organizational plan** should be determined. Some considerations include: What basic background information does the reader (the audience) need to understand the topic? What is the basis of the ideas to be presented? In other words, what topics need to be explained first so the reader will understand other topics? What is the most logical way to present the information? Readers tend to prefer that one topic lead to the next. Organizational plans detail the characteristics, causes, effects, sequences of events, similarities, and contrasts.

A sample organizational plan for the Emily Dickinson research example could involve presenting in the first section a historical account of the nineteenth-century women's rights movement and a definition of the concept of feminism during Dickinson's life. The next sections could cover the main feminist ideas Dickinson expressed in her poetry.

Once an organizational plan is outlined, the researcher should start taking **notes** from the sources gathered. Most important, each note must include identifying information about the source, including publication details and page numbers. In addition, the section of the outline that corresponds with the source information noted must be designated above each note. This way, the notes are categorized according to the outline, or organizational plan.

Notes come in four different forms. A **direct quotation** is three or more consecutive words copied precisely from a source. It must be designated by quotation marks or by block indentation if the quotation is longer than four lines of prose or three lines of poetry. A quotation can be a definition or a well-worded or authoritative statement that will amplify a main point.

A **paraphrase** is a reworded version of any sentence in a source. Typically, a sentence with complex or sophisticated wording needs to be paraphrased. The main thoughts are pulled apart, and the language is simplified, but the original meaning is retained.

A **summary** is a shortened version of a section of a source, containing only the main points or events of the original. Any type of descriptive, detailed, or narrative text, such as news stories, fictional stories, or chronicles of events needs to be summed up.

An **idea and list**—the most common form of notes—consists of the key idea of a section of text followed by a bulleted list of related details. Again, all notes should be marked with corresponding outline sections, so it will be easy to put the notes in the order of the outline and use the information to compose the paper.

The following are sample notes for research on feminist ideas expressed by Emily Dickinson:

Cooper, Susan Fenimore. "Female Suffrage: A Letter to the Christian Women of America." *Harper's New Weekly Magazine* XLI (June–November 1870): 594–600.

Outline Section I

Three Reasons Women Remain in a Subordinate Position:

1. They are physically weaker and depend on men for protection.
2. They are intellectually inferior.
   ▷ This claim is considered debatable.
   ▷ Why women have not educated themselves is of concern.
3. Christianity teaches that men are the head of the household.
   ▷ But protects her more than other systems

Figure 2.1.a Primary Source

Dickinson, Emily. "My Life had stood – a Loaded Gun." Stanzas 1–3.

Outline Section I

My life had stood—a Loaded Gun—
In Corners—till a Day
The Owner passed—identified—
And carried Me away—

And now We roam in Sovereign Woods—
And now We hurt the Doe—
And every time I speak for Him—
The Mountains straight reply—
And do I smile, such cordial light
Upon the Valley glow—
It is as a Vesuvian face
Had let its pleasure through—

Figure 2.1.b Primary Source

Rich, Adrienne. "Vesuvius at Home: The Power of Emily Dickinson." Reprinted in *Literary Theories in Praxis*. Edited by Shirley F. Staton. Philadelphia: University of Pennsylvania Press, 1987. pp. 258 – 59.

Outline Section I

Speaking of Emily Dickinson's poem "My Life had stood – a Loaded Gun," Adrienne Rich explains, "But I think that for us, at this time, it is a central poem in understanding Emily Dickinson, and ourselves, and the condition of the woman artist, particularly in the nineteenth century. It seems likely that the nineteenth-century woman poet, especially, felt the medium of poetry as dangerous…. Poetry is too much rooted in the unconscious; it presses too close against the barriers of repression; and the nineteenth-century woman had much to repress."

Paraphrase of the above quotation:

Nineteenth-century women had to repress many of their thoughts. In other words, they pushed these thoughts into their unconscious minds and weren't aware of them. Since the unconscious mind is the source of poetic expression, writing poetry was dangerous for a nineteenth-century woman; in doing so, she gave expression to these repressed thoughts and feelings.

Figure 2.2. Secondary Source

SAMPLE QUESTIONS

26) **Which of the following is an example of a secondary source for an article on local highways?**

    A.   an online opinion column promoting tax incentives for those who carpool

    B.   photographs of traffic accidents

    C.   data from the city's transportation department

    D.   an autobiography of a city official who led efforts to improve local infrastructure

    E.   emails about highway congestion sent to the mayor

27) **What is a good reason for a writer of a research paper to include a short section of text copied word for word from a source?**

    A.   The text is a secondary source.

    B.   The vocabulary is sophisticated.

    C.   The text is well worded.

    D.   The information relates to several areas of the research.

    E.   The section of text would take a significant amount of time to paraphrase.

CITATIONS

In general, any ideas or details that are not original to the writer must be documented. Specifically, this includes any information quoted, paraphrased, or summarized from sources.

Information taken from sources is documented with **in-text citations**, **internal documentation**, or **parenthetical references**. These terms are used interchangeably to mean that the source information—usually the author's last name or the first main words of the title plus the page, line, or section number—is put in parentheses right after the paraphrase, quotation, or summary. If the source of the information is introduced in the text with the author's name, the writer puts just the page, line, or section number in the parentheses.

Citations show the reader what sources the writer used for research. They also guide the reader to more information on topics covered in a text.

SAMPLE QUESTION

28) **Why are citations useful to the reader?**
   A. They provide interesting information for the reader.
   B. They show that the author did not plagiarize.
   C. They guide the reader to more information on a topic.
   D. They help readers better understand the text by providing extra information.
   E. They prove the validity of a text.

ANSWER KEY

1) A.   Incorrect. The pronoun "you" does not make sense here. It is the writer's car that is in the shop, not a different person.

   B.   Correct. The pronoun "I" refers to the writer. It agrees with the verb "could use." The pronouns "me" and "mine" also refer to the writer, so first-person singular makes the most sense.

   C.   Incorrect. "My" is a possessive pronoun. It cannot function as the subject of a verb (here, "could use").

   D.   Incorrect. "His" is a possessive pronoun. It cannot act as the subject of a verb. It also does not make sense in this sentence.

   E.   Incorrect. The pronoun "us" is an object pronoun. It cannot function as the subject of the verb "could use."

2) **A.   Correct.** The singular indefinite pronoun "everybody" agrees with the singular verb "believes" and makes sense in this sentence.

   B.   Incorrect. The indefinite pronoun "something" does agree in number with the singular verb "believes," but it does not make sense in the sentence.

   C.   Incorrect. The singular verb "believes" does not agree with the plural pronoun "several."

   D.   Incorrect. The plural indefinite pronoun "few" does not agree with the singular verb "believes."

   E.   Incorrect. Again, the plural indefinite pronoun "many" does not agree with the singular verb "believes."

3) **C.   Correct.** This sentence requires the future perfect tense because the speaker is talking about an event that will be conducted and completed in the future.

4) **A.   Correct.** The intransitive verb "sit" is used incorrectly here. The writer should have used the transitive verb "set," which means "to put" or "to set something" down, like plates on a table.

5) **D.   Correct.** Choice D should read "Of the four speeches, Jerry's was the longest." The word "long" has only one syllable, so it should be modified with the suffix –*est*, not the word "most."

6) **D.   Correct.** This is a sentence fragment that begins with the subordinating conjunction "because." There is no independent clause.

7) **E.   Correct.** Prepositions establish relationships in space (or time). This sentence describes a spatial relationship, so it needs a preposition about space or direction. The preposition "to" clarifies the relationship between the speaker, the ball, and the speaker's friend: the speaker is throwing the ball *to* the friend.

8) **A.** **Correct.** This choice is not a complete sentence. Rather, it is a combination of two phrases: a noun phrase ("Ten cats") and a prepositional phrase ("in a row"). There is no verb and no predicate.

9) **D.** **Correct.** This is a sentence fragment. It is a dependent clause beginning with a subordinating conjunction, "whenever." It contains a subject, "I," and a predicate, "visit," but there is no independent clause attached to the dependent clause. Therefore, it cannot act as a full sentence.

10) **A.** **Correct.** The first clause is dependent and the second is independent, so they are correctly joined by a comma.

11) **D.** **Correct.** A colon can be used to introduce a list.

12) **B.** **Correct.** This compound sentence requires a comma before the conjunction "but."

13) **C)** **Correct.** "Spring" is the name of a season and should not be capitalized.

14) **B.** **Correct.** The verb agrees with the closest subject—in this case, the singular "brother."

15) **A.** **Correct.** "Grandchildren" and "cousins" are plural and so take the plural pronoun "their."

16) **B.** **Correct.** This sentence contains a dangling modifier. Who is allergic to bananas? Probably Donna, but "smoothies" appears next to the modifying phase "being allergic to bananas." The writer probably means that Donna is allergic to bananas, but this sentence is written in a confusing manner and contains a structural error.

17) **D.** **Correct.** This choice creates a comma splice. The other choices are all correct.

18) **B.** **Correct.** This sentence does not use parallel structure. A better version would be "I love running, swimming, and hiking, but I hate camping."

19) A. Incorrect. This group of words is not a complete thought and would be considered a fragment.

    B. **Correct.** This sentence joins two complete thoughts with only a comma and would therefore be classified as a comma splice.

    C. Incorrect. This sentence correctly joins a dependent and independent clause using a comma.

    D. Incorrect. This sentence is punctuated properly and constructed correctly.

    E. Incorrect. This sentence correctly uses commas to join three items in a list.

20) A.   Incorrect. This sentence is still redundant; a surprise is, by definition, unexpected.

B.   **Correct.** This concise rewrite expresses the idea without any redundancy or grammatical errors.

C.   Incorrect. This choice contains both redundancy and a grammatical error (a comma splice).

D.   Incorrect. This sentence is clumsy. It is needlessly wordy, though there is no redundancy.

E.   Incorrect. This sentence contains a redundancy ("shocked and surprised").

21) D.   **Correct.** The word "affect" is used incorrectly here. The correct usage is "effect."

22) A.   **Correct.** The content agrees with what other reliable sources on the topic indicate.

B.   Incorrect. The writer's background may be clear, but that background is not the subject of the source.

C.   Incorrect. A respected organization is unrelated to scholarly research, an author's qualifications, or the use of verifiable data.

D.   Incorrect. The writer may be a journalist or admired, but that does not mean the writer is knowledgeable about the subject of the text or has collected data that supports the ideas of the source.

E.   Incorrect. Although the perspective should be clear, it has to be supported by reliable data.

23) A.   Incorrect. A quality source has citations, quotations, footnotes, and a works-cited page.

B.   Incorrect. A peer-reviewed source has been assessed by scholars who have credentials in the same area as the author of the source.

C.   Incorrect. A quality source may be a recent publication.

D.   **Correct.** The author of a quality source is an expert in the source's area of study and will have included or cited relevant information from other authorities on the topic.

E.   Incorrect. Providing relevant explanations is helpful, but not if such explanations come only from a popular perspective. A perspective must be based on verifiable fact.

24) A.   **Correct.** A secondary source is a written analysis or interpretation of a primary source. Examples include literary and historical criticism.

B.   Incorrect. This option describes a primary source.

C.   Incorrect. This is a possibility, but it does not define what a secondary source is.

D.   Incorrect. These are possibilities, but they do not explain what a secondary source is.

E.   Incorrect. This option is more applicable to a primary source; however, secondary sources may refer to interviews or surveys reported in primary sources.

25) A.   Incorrect. A secondary source is a written analysis or interpretation of a primary source. Examples include literary and historical criticism.

B.   Incorrect. The speaker may not be authoritative or even knowledgeable.

C.   Incorrect. This is possible but hopefully not true.

D.   Incorrect. Some political speeches may include an anecdote or follow a narrative structure. However, this option does not define or categorize a political speech.

E.   Correct. Primary sources are firsthand accounts of a topic. They are created by authors who have direct experience with the subject and are usually created at the time the authors are involved with the subject. A political speech is written or given by a person who is directly involved with the issues presented in the speech.

26) A.   Correct. Only this option describes a secondary source, since it offers analysis of a topic, not firsthand experience of it.

B.   Incorrect. Photographs are a primary source.

C.   Incorrect. The analysis or interpretation of data could be considered a secondary source, but the data itself is a primary source.

D.   Incorrect. An autobiography is a primary source.

E.   Incorrect. Emails are a primary source.

27) A.   Incorrect. The type of source does not affect whether a direct quote should be included in a research paper.

B.   Incorrect. Sophisticated vocabulary is not a good enough reason to quote text; the text should still be paraphrased.

C.   Correct. Quoting a statement with emphatic or memorable wording can be an especially effective way to amplify an argument in a research paper.

D.   Incorrect. Ideally all the information in a research paper is relevant, so this is not a reason to include direct quotations.

E.   Incorrect. The amount of work it would take to write the research paper is not a factor in whether to include direct quotes.

28) A.   Incorrect. Citations may be interesting to some readers, but their true value is as a roadmap for further research. They provide readers the names of authors, texts, and resources to study for more information on a topic.

B.   Incorrect. Citations can show that an author properly attributed his or her work, but this is not their primary purpose for a reader.

C. **Correct.** Citations' primary benefit is that they provide more information for readers to research topics of interest.

D. Incorrect. Footnotes and endnotes usually provide extra information to enhance understanding, not citations.

E. Citations by themselves do not prove a text is valid. If a writer used unreliable sources and properly cited them, the sources are still unreliable.

3

Mathematics

NUMBER AND QUANTITY

TYPES OF NUMBERS

Numbers can be classified into various groups based on their properties.

▶ **Natural numbers** are the numbers used to count objects: 1, 2, 3, 4, …

▶ **Whole numbers** include all the natural numbers and 0.

▶ **Integers** include 0, the natural numbers (also called positive numbers), and their opposites, the negative integers (–1, –2, –3, …).

▶ **Positive numbers** are greater than 0, and **negative numbers** are less than 0. Both positive and negative numbers can be shown on a number line.

◀———————————————————————————▶
  –10 –9 –8 –7 –6 –5 –4 –3 –2 –1 0 1 2 3 4 5 6 7 8 9 10

Figure 3.1. Number Line

▶ **Rational numbers** are defined as any number that can be written as a fraction (a part over a whole, such as $\frac{3}{4}$). Rational numbers include all integers and the fractional values between them.

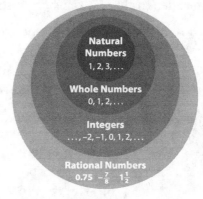

Figure 3.2. Types of Numbers

SAMPLE QUESTION

1) A student claims that "all integers are also whole numbers." Which of the following numbers is a counterexample to the student's claim?

    A.   −5
    B.   0
    C. $\frac{2}{3}$
    D.   1
    E.   100

BASIC OPERATIONS

The four basic arithmetic operations are addition, subtraction, multiplication, and division.

> **HELPFUL HINT**
>
> The absolute value of a number is the number without a sign.

Add (+) to combine two quantities. The quantities being added are called the **addends**. **Subtract** (−) to find the difference of two quantities. Subtraction is the opposite of addition.

▶   If the numbers have the same sign, add their absolute values and give the answer the same sign.

$$-2 + (-7) = -9$$

▶   If the numbers have different signs, subtract their absolute values. Then give the answer the sign of the number with the largest absolute value.

$$4 + (-9) = -5$$

▶   To subtract two numbers, change the sign of the second number and add.

$$6 - 11 = 6 + (-11) = -5$$
$$12 - (-10) = 12 + 10 = 22$$

Addition can also be visualized on a number line. Start with the first addend, then move to the right or left depending on the sign of the second addend.

> **HELPFUL HINT**
>
> The **remainder** is what is left over when one number does not divide evenly into another. For example, when 13 is divided by 4 ($13 \div 4$ or $\frac{13}{4}$), there is a remainder of 1.

Multiply (×) to add a quantity multiple times (e.g., $6 \times 3 = 6 + 6 + 6 = 18$). The numbers being multiplied together are called **factors**. **Divide** (÷) to find out how many times one quantity goes into another. Division is the opposite of multiplication.

▶   If the signs are the same, make the answer positive.

$$-3 \times -4 = 12$$

▶ If the signs are different, make the answer negative.

$$-30 \div 10 = -3$$

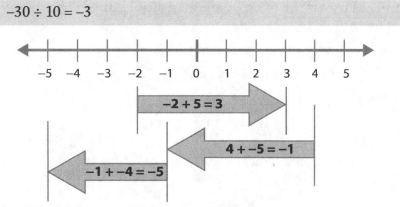

Figure 3.3. Adding Positive and Negative Numbers

SAMPLE QUESTIONS

2) **The temperature on a cold day in January was −3°F. When the sun went down, the temperature fell 5 degrees. What was the temperature after the sun went down?**

   A.   −15°F

   B.   −8°F

   C.   0°F

   D.   2°F

   E.   15°F

3) **A case of pencils contains 24 boxes. Each box contains 110 pencils. How many pencils are in the case?**

   A.   86

   B.   134

   C.   2640

   D.   5280

   E.   290,400

EXPONENTS AND RADICALS

Exponential expressions, such as 5^3, contain a base and an exponent. The **exponent** indicates how many times to use the **base** as a factor. In the expression 5^3, 5 is the base, and 3 is the exponent. The value of 5^3 is found by multiplying 5 by itself 3 times:

$$5^3 = 5 \times 5 \times 5 = 125$$

Finding the **root** of a number is the inverse of raising a number to a power. In other words, the root is the number of times a value should be multiplied by itself to reach a given value. Roots are named for the power on the base:

▶ 5 is the **square root** of 25, because $5^2 = 25$

▶ 5 is the **cube root** of 125, because $5^3 = 125$

▶ 5 is the **fourth root** of 625, because $5^4 = 625$

The symbol for finding the root of a number is the radical: $\sqrt{\square}$. By itself, the radical indicates a square root: $\sqrt{36} = 6$ because $6^2 = 36$. Other numbers can be included in front of the radical to indicate different roots: $\sqrt[4]{1296} = 6$ because $6^4 = 1296$.

SAMPLE QUESTIONS

4)   Which of the following is equivalent to 64?

A. 2^3

B. 2^4

C. 4^3

D. 4^4

E. 4^5

5)   Which of the following is equivalent to $\sqrt{100}$?

A.   2.5

B.   5

C.   10

D.   25

E.   1000

ORDER OF OPERATIONS

The **order of operations** is a set of rules for simplifying expressions that include more than one operation. The rules describe the order in which operations should be performed:

1.   **Parentheses**—Perform operations within parentheses or other grouping symbols, such as brackets.

2.   **Exponents**—Simplify exponential expressions.

3.   **Multiplication and division**—Work multiplication and division from left to right. Multiplication does not necessarily come before division.

4.   **Addition and subtraction**—Work addition and subtraction from left to right. Addition does not necessarily come before subtraction.

The acronym **PEMDAS** is often used to remember the order of operations.

SAMPLE QUESTION

6)   Which of the following is equivalent to $7 + 24 \div 8 \times (4 - 6)^2$?

    A.   1

    B.   15.5

    C.   19

    D.   40

    E.   90.25

PROPERTIES OF WHOLE NUMBERS

Every whole number (except 1) is either a prime number or a composite number.

▶   A **prime number** is a natural number greater than 1 that can be divided evenly only by 1 and itself. For example, 7 is a prime number because it is divisible only by 1 and 7.

▶   A **composite number** is a natural number greater than 1 that can be evenly divided by at least one other number besides 1 and itself. For example, 6 is a composite number because it can be divided by 1, 2, 3, and 6.

Composite numbers can be broken down into **factors**: the numbers that are multiplied together to produce the composite number. Factors can be found by finding all the sets of multiples that produce the composite number. The example below shows all the factors of 54.

$$54 = 54 \times 1$$
$$54 = 27 \times 2$$
$$54 = 18 \times 3$$
$$54 = 9 \times 6$$
The factors of 54 are 1, 2, 3, 6, 9, 18, 27, and 54.

Figure 3.4 shows how the number 54 can be broken down into prime factors: $54 = 2 \times 3 \times 3 \times 3$.

The **greatest common factor (GCF)** of a set of numbers, also called the **greatest common divisor**, is the greatest number (other than 1) that each number in the set is divisible by without any remainders. The GCF may be one of the numbers; for example, for the numbers 4 and 8, the GCF is 4, since 4 goes into both 4 and 8.

The **least common multiple (LCM)** of a set of numbers is the smallest number that is a multiple of all the numbers in the set. The LCM is often called the **least common denominator (LCD)**, especially when it is used to add and subtract fractions. To find the LCM of numbers, write out all the multiples and

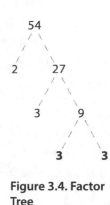

Figure 3.4. Factor Tree

HELPFUL HINT

Even numbers are multiples of 2, meaning they have 2 as a factor (2, 4, 6, . . .).

Odd numbers have a remainder when divided by 2.

look for the smallest number that is in both lists.

6: 6, 12, 18, **24**, 30
8: 8, 16, **24**, 32
The least common multiple of 6 and 8 is 24.

SAMPLE QUESTION

7) **In the Venn diagram below, circle A represents all the factors of 12 and circle B represents all the factors of 26. How many numbers are included in the shaded region?**

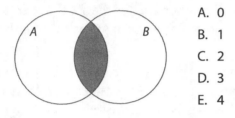

 A. 0

 B. 1

 C. 2

 D. 3

 E. 4

FRACTIONS

A **fraction** represents parts of a whole. The top number of a fraction, called the **numerator**, indicates how many equal-sized parts are present. The bottom number of a fraction, called the **denominator**, indicates how many equal-sized parts make a whole.

Fractions have several forms:

▶ **proper fraction**: the numerator is less than the denominator

▶ **improper fraction**: the numerator is greater than or equal to the denominator

▶ **mixed number**: the combination of a whole number and a fraction

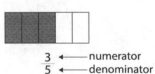

Figure 3.5. Parts of a Fraction

Improper fractions can be converted to mixed numbers by dividing. (The fraction bar is also a division symbol.) The remainder becomes the new numerator.

$$\frac{9}{4} = 2\frac{1}{4}$$

To convert a mixed number to a fraction, multiply the whole number by the denominator of the fraction, and add the numerator. The result becomes the numerator of the improper fraction; the denominator remains the same.

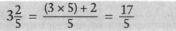

$$3\frac{2}{5} = \frac{(3 \times 5) + 2}{5} = \frac{17}{5}$$

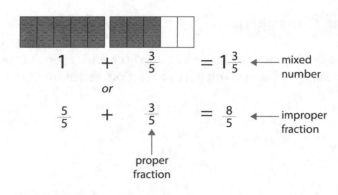

Figure 3.6. Types of Fractions

Adding or subtracting fractions requires a **common denominator**. This value may be the least common denominator. However, the easiest way to find a common denominator is simply to multiply all the denominators together.

Multiply each fraction by the value needed to create a common denominator. Once all the denominators are the same, add or subtract the numerators.

> **HELPFUL HINT**
>
> To create **equivalent fractions** (fractions that are equal), multiply the numerator and denominator by the same number.

$$\frac{3}{10} + \frac{2}{3} = \left(\frac{3}{3}\right)\frac{3}{10} + \left(\frac{10}{10}\right)\frac{2}{3} = \frac{9}{30} + \frac{20}{30} = \frac{29}{30}$$

$$\frac{3}{5} - \frac{1}{4} = \left(\frac{4}{4}\right)\frac{3}{5} - \left(\frac{5}{5}\right)\frac{1}{4} = \frac{12}{20} - \frac{5}{20} = \frac{7}{20}$$

A common denominator is not necessary for multiplication or division of fractions. To **multiply fractions**, multiply numerators and multiply denominators. Reduce the product to lowest terms.

$$5/6 \times 2/3 = (5 \times 2)/(6 \times 3) = 10/18 = 5/9$$

To **divide fractions**, multiply the first fraction by the reciprocal of the second fraction. To find the **reciprocal** of a fraction, swap the numerator and the denominator.

$$2/3 \div 1/4 = 2/3 \times 4/1 = 8/3$$

When multiplying and dividing mixed numbers, the mixed numbers must be converted to improper fractions.

$$2\ 3/7 \times 1/2 = 17/7 \times 1/2 = 17/14$$

SAMPLE QUESTIONS

8)   Carla divides her pizza into 8 equal slices and takes 1 piece. If the amount of pizza remaining is written as a fraction, the numerator will be:

A.   0

B.   1

C.   7

D.   8

E.   9

9)   A student is taking a survey of her classmates for a project. She finds that $\frac{3}{4}$ of students have a favorite book. Of the students who have a favorite book, $\frac{1}{5}$ say that *The Hunger Games* is their favorite book. What fraction of the total class says that *The Hunger Games* is their favorite book?

DECIMALS

Decimal numbers use decimal notation to express fractions with denominators that are powers of ten. Each digit to the right of the decimal point has a place value of tenths, hundredths, thousandths, and so on. For example, the fraction $\frac{319}{1000}$ written in decimal notation would be 0.319.

Table 3.1. Place Value Chart

1,000,000	100,000	10,000	1,000	100	10	1		1/10	1/100
10^6	10^5	10^4	10^3	10^2	10^1	10^0	.	10^{-1}	10^{-2}
millions	hundred thousands	ten thousands	thousands	hundreds	tens	ones	decimal	tenths	hundredths

To convert a decimal number to a fraction, write the digits in the numerator and write the place value of the final digit in the denominator. Reduce to lowest terms, if necessary.

TEST TIP	
The Praxis exam includes an on-screen calculator that will allow you to easily add, subtract, multiply, and divide decimal numbers.	$0.092 = \frac{92}{1000} = \frac{92 \div 4}{1000 \div 4} = \frac{23}{250}$ To convert a fraction to a decimal, divide the numerator by the denominator. $\frac{5}{8} = 5 \div 8 = 0.625$

Rounding is used to make numbers easier to work with. The process makes numbers less accurate, but the operations and mental math are easier.

To round a number, first identify the digit in the specified place (such as the tenths or hundredths). Then look at the digit one place to the right. If that digit is four or less, keep the digit in the specified place the same. If that digit is five or more, add 1 to the digit in the specified place. All the digits to the right of the specified place become zeros.

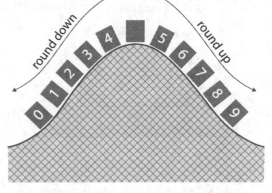

Figure 3.7. Rounding

Numbers can be rounded to any place value:

▶ rounded to the hundreds place: 5372 → 5400

▶ rounded to the tenths place: 11.635 → 11.600

SAMPLE QUESTIONS

10) **Which digit is in the hundredths place when 1.3208 is divided by 5.2?**

  A. 0

  B. 2

  C. 4

  D. 5

  E. 8

11) **What is 498,235 rounded to the nearest thousands?**

  A. 498,000

  B. 498,200

  C. 499,000

  D. 499,200

  E. 500,000

ORDERING NUMBERS

Some questions on the Math exam may require that numbers be compared or placed in ascending order. Below are some methods that can help make ordering numbers easier.

▶ For sets with fractions, give all the fractions a common denominator.

▶ For sets with fractions and decimals, convert all fractions to decimals. (Use the on-screen calculator if needed.)

▶ Place the numbers on a number line to visualize their relationship.

SAMPLE QUESTION

12) **Which of the following numbers would create a list of numbers ordered from least to greatest if inserted in the blank space?**

$\frac{1}{2}$, _____, 0.825

A.   1.5

B.   0

C. $\frac{1}{3}$

D.   −0.75

E. $\frac{4}{5}$

RATIOS AND PROPORTIONS

A **ratio** is a comparison of two quantities. For example, if a class consists of 15 women and 10 men, the ratio of women to men is 15 to 10. This ratio can also be written as 15:10 or $\frac{15}{10}$. Ratios, like fractions, can be reduced. To **reduce** a fraction or ratio, divide each number by the largest factor they share.

$$\frac{25}{15} = \frac{25 \div 5}{15 \div 5} = \frac{5}{3}$$

A **proportion** is a statement that two ratios are equal. For example, proportion $\frac{5}{10} = \frac{7}{14}$ is true because both ratios are equal to $\frac{1}{2}$.

Proportions have a useful quality: their cross-products are equal. For the example proportion above:

$$\frac{5}{10} = \frac{7}{14}$$
$$5(14) = 7(10)$$
$$70 = 70$$

HELPFUL HINT

Cross product:

$\frac{a}{b} = \frac{c}{d} \rightarrow ad = bc$

The fact that the cross-products of proportions are equal can be used to solve proportions in which one of the values is missing. (See Algebra and its subsections later in this chapter to learn how to solve simple algebraic equations.)

$$\frac{6}{13} = \frac{x}{39}$$
$$13x = 6(39)$$
$$13x = 234$$
$$x = 18$$

13) A company employs 30 people, 12 of whom are men. What is the ratio of women to men working at the company?

_____

14) The dosage for a particular medication is proportional to the weight of the patient. If the dosage for a patient weighing 60 kg is 90 mg, what is the dosage for a patient weighing 80 kg?

A.   40 mg

B.   120 mg

C.   160 mg

D.   180 mg

E.   7200 mg

Percentages

A **percent** (or percentage) means *per hundred* and is expressed with the percent symbol, %. For example, 54% means 54 out of every 100. Percentages are turned into decimals by moving the decimal point two places to the left, so 54% = 0.54. Percentages can be solved by setting up a proportion:

HELPFUL HINT
Key words for percent increase: "markup," "growth," "increased." Key words for percent decrease: "marked down," "sale," "decreased."

$$\frac{part}{whole} = \frac{\%}{100}$$

Percent change describes how much a value has increased or decreased. It is found using the formula:

$$percent\ change = \frac{new\ amount - old\ amount}{old\ amount} \times 100$$

To find the amount that a value has changed, it's often easier to use the formula given below, where percent change is given as a decimal:

$$amount\ of\ change = original\ amount \times percent\ change$$

15) 16 is 80% of what number?

_____

16) **A store owner buys 100 textbooks for $16 per book. If he marks up each book by 8% and sells all the books, what will his profit be?**

 A. $128

 B. $160

 C. $168

 D. $1600

 E. $1728

UNITS

The United States uses **customary units**, sometimes called standard units. Most countries use the **metric system**, which uses a different set of units.

Table 3.2. US Customary Units

Dimension	Customary Units	Metric Units	Converting Between Customary Units	Converting Between Customary and Metric Units
length	inch (in) foot (ft) yard (yd) mile (mi)	meter (m)	12 inches = 1 foot 3 feet = 1 yard 5280 feet = 1 mile	1 in = 2.54 cm 1 ft = 0.3 m 1 yd = 0.914 m 1 mi = 1.61 km
mass	ounce (oz) pound (lb)	gram (g)	16 ounces = 1 pound 2000 pounds = 1 ton	1 oz = 28.35 g 1 lb = 0.454 kg
volume	fluid ounce (fl oz) cup (c) pint (pt) quart (qt) gallon (gal)	liter (L)	8 fluid ounces = 1 cup 2 cups = 1 pint 2 pints = 1 quart 4 quarts = 1 gallon	1 gal = 3.785 L

The metric system also uses a set of prefixes to make it easier to express very large and very small measurements. The prefixes are added to the unit.

1000 meters = 1 kilometer
1000 m = 1 km

Table 3.3. Metric Prefixes

Prefix	Symbol	Multiplication Factor
tera	T	1,000,000,000,000
giga	G	1,000,000,000
mega	M	1,000,000

Prefix	Symbol	Multiplication Factor
kilo	k	1,000
hecto	h	100
deca	da	10
base unit	--	--
deci	d	0.1
centi	c	0.01
milli	m	0.001
micro	µ	0.0000001
nano	n	0.0000000001
pico	p	0.0000000000001

Units can be converted within the customary system and between the two systems using dimensional analysis. Start with the original unit and multiply by the conversion factor (written as a fraction like $\frac{1000 \text{ m}}{1 \text{ km}}$) to get the new unit. Note that units that appear on the top and bottom cancel out.

$$\frac{120 \text{ in}}{\square} \times \frac{1 \text{ ft}}{12 \text{ in}} = 10 \text{ ft}$$

$$6 \text{ m/s} = \frac{6 \text{ m}}{1 \text{ s}} \times \frac{1 \text{ ft}}{0.3 \text{ m}} = \frac{6 \text{ ft}}{0.3 \text{ s}} = 20 \text{ ft/s}$$

A similar strategy can be used to solve problems that involve a rate, such as meters per second or miles per hour. These problems will ask for quantities like distance or time. Place the standalone value on the left, and multiply by the rate.

How long will it take a car traveling 60 miles per hour to travel 300 miles?

$$\frac{300 \text{ miles}}{\square} \times \frac{1 \text{ hour}}{60 \text{ miles}} = 5 \text{ hours}$$

SAMPLE QUESTIONS

17) **Which of the following is an appropriate unit for measuring the height of an adult?**

    A.   pound

    B.   kilometer

    C.   liter

    D.   mile

    E.   meter

18) A 10,000-gallon pool is being filled at a rate of x gallons per minute. Which of the following expressions describes the length of time in minutes it will take for the pool to be full?

A. $10,000x$

B. $\frac{10,000}{x}$

C. $10,000 + x$

D. $\frac{10,000 + x}{x}$

E. $x - 10,000$

Data Interpretation and Representation, Statistics, and Probability

Measures of Central Tendency

Measures of central tendency help identify the center, or most typical, value within a data set. There are three such central tendencies that describe the "center" of the data in different ways. The **mean** (μ) is the arithmetic average and is found by dividing the sum of all measurements by the number of measurements.

$$\mu = \frac{x_1 + x_2 + \dots x_N}{N}$$

Find the mean of the following data set: {75, 62, 78, 92, 83, 90}

$$\frac{75 + 62 + 78 + 92 + 83 + 90}{6} = \frac{480}{6} = 80$$

The **median** divides a set into two equal halves. To calculate the median, place the data set in ascending order. The median is the measurement right in the middle of an odd set of measurements or the average of the two middle numbers in an even data set.

Find the median of the following data set: {2, 15, 16, 8, 21, 13, 4}
Place the data in ascending order: {2, 4, 8, 13, 15, 16, 21}
The median is the value in the middle: 13

Find the median of the following data set: {75, 62, 78, 92, 83, 91}
Place the data in ascending order:
{62, 75, 78, 83, 91, 92}
Find the average of the two middle values: $(78 + 83)/2 = 80.5$

HELPFUL HINT

Adding a constant to each value in a data set will change both the mean and median by that value. Multiplying each value in a set by a constant will also change the mean and median by the same value.

Outliers are values in a data set that are much larger or smaller than the other values in the set. Outliers can skew the mean, making it higher or lower than most of the values. The median is not affected by outliers, so it is a better measure of central tendency when outliers are present.

> **For the set {3, 5, 10, 12, 65}:**
>
> $$\text{mean} = \frac{3 + 5 + 10 + 12 + 65}{5} = 19$$
>
> $$\text{median} = 10$$
>
> The outlier (65) drags the mean much higher than the median.

The **mode** is simply the measurement that occurs most often. There can be one, several, or no modes in a data set.

SAMPLE QUESTION

19) **A student has an average of 81 on four equally weighted tests she has taken in her statistics class. She wants to determine what grade she must receive on her fifth test so that her mean is 83. What grade must she receive on her fifth test?**

   A.   81

   B.   83

   C.   85

   D.   89

   E.   91

MEASURES OF DISPERSION

The values in a data set can be very close together (close to the mean) or very spread out. This is called the **spread** or **dispersion** of the data. There are a few **measures of dispersion** that quantify the spread within a data set. **Range** is the difference between the largest and smallest data points in a set:

> R = largest data point – smallest data point

Notice range depends on only two data points, the two extremes. Sometimes these data points are outliers; regardless, for a large data set, relying on only two data points is not an exact tool. To better understand the data set, calculate **quartiles**, which divide data sets into four equally sized groups. To calculate quartiles:

1. Arrange the data in ascending order.
2. Find the set's median (also called quartile 2 or Q2).
3. Find the median of the lower half of the data, called quartile 1 (Q1).
4. Find the median of the upper half of the data, called quartile 3 (Q3).

The interquartile range (IQR) provides a more reliable range that is not as affected by extremes. IQR is the difference between the third quartile data point and the first quartile data point:

$$IQR = Q_3 - Q_1$$

SAMPLE QUESTION

20) **The table below shows the number of customers that came into a restaurant each day of the week. What is the range of the data set?**

Day of the Week	Number of Customers
Monday	72
Tuesday	89
Wednesday	125
Thursday	212
Friday	350
Saturday	418
Sunday	262

Types of Graphs

Bar graphs present the numbers of an item that exist in different categories. The categories are shown on one axis, and the number of items is shown on the other axis. Bar graphs are usually used to compare amounts easily.

Histograms similarly use bars to compare data, but the independent variable is a continuous variable that has been "binned" or divided into categories. For example, the time of day can be broken down into 8:00 a.m. to 12:00 p.m., 12:00

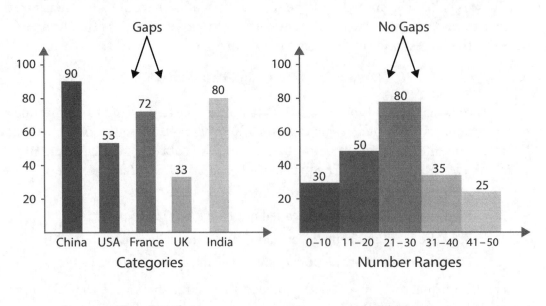

Bar Graph   **Histogram**

Figure 3.8. Bar Graph versus Histogram

p.m. to 4:00 p.m., and so on. Usually (but not always), a gap is included between the bars of a bar graph but not a histogram.

Scatter plots show the relationship between two sets of data by plotting the data as ordered pairs (x, y). One variable is plotted along the horizontal axis, and the second variable is plotted along the vertical axis.

The data in a scatter plot may show a **linear relationship** between the data sets. (See "Linear Relationships" later in the chapter for more information on modeling linear relationships algebraically.) There is a **positive correlation** (expressed as a positive slope) if increasing one variable corresponds to an increase in the other variable. A **negative correlation** (expressed as a negative slope) occurs when an increase in one variable corresponds to a decrease in the other. If the scatter plot shows no discernible pattern, then there is no correlation (a zero, mixed, or indiscernible slope).

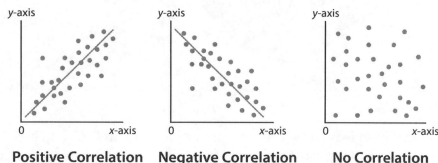

Positive Correlation   **Negative Correlation**   **No Correlation**

Figure 3.9. Scatter Plots and Correlation

Correlation is a mathematical term that describes two variables that are statistically related (meaning one variable can be used to predict the other). **Causation** means that one variable directly influences another through a known mechanism. Correlation is not the same as causation: knowing two variables are statistically related does not mean one is directly influencing the other.

HELPFUL HINT

In a line graph, each x-value corresponds to exactly one y-value. A scatter plot may have multiple y-values for one x-value.

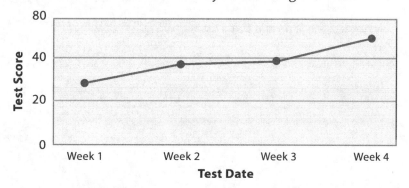

Figure 3.10. Line Graph

Line graphs are used to display a relationship between two continuous variables, such as change over time. Line graphs are constructed by graphing each point and connecting each point to the next consecutive point by a line.

Pie charts show parts of a whole and are often used with percentages. Together, all the slices of the pie add up to the total number of items, or 100%.

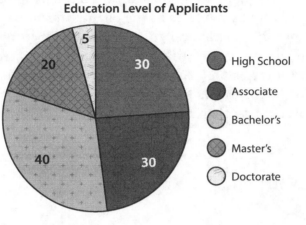

Figure 3.11. Pie Chart

Stem-and-leaf plots are ways of organizing large amounts of data by grouping it into rows. All data points are broken into two parts: a stem and a leaf. For instance, the number 512 might be broken into a stem of 5 and a leaf of 12. All data in the 500 range would appear in the same row (this group of data is a class). The advantage of this display is that it shows general density and shape of the data in a compact display, yet all original data points are preserved and available. It is also easy to find medians and quartiles from this display.

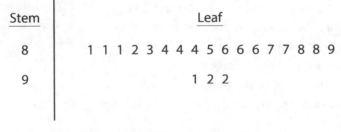

Figure 3.12. Stem and Leaf Plot

SAMPLE QUESTIONS

21) The graph below shows the average high temperature in Houston, Texas, for each month.

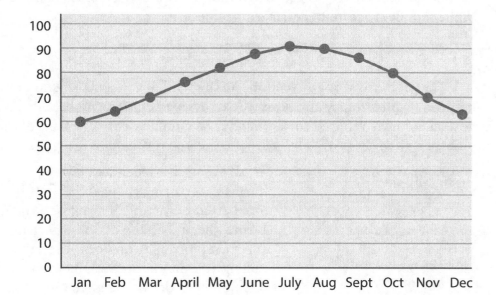

Which of the following is closest to the range for this data set?

A. 5

B. 15

C. 30

D. 60

E. 90

22) The stem-and-leaf plot below shows students' scores on a recent math test.

9	9, 8, 8, 5, 2, 1
8	8, 8, 8, 4, 2
7	9, 8, 6, 2
6	7, 7, 3
5	5

9|9 = 99

What was the median student score on the test?

A. 65

B. 84

C. 82

D. 88

E. 91

PROBABILITY

Probability (*P*) is the likelihood of one or a certain number of specific events occurring. The probability of a single event occurring is the number of outcomes in which that event occurs (called **favorable events**) divided by the number of items in the **sample space** (total possible outcomes):

$$P(\text{an event}) = \frac{\text{number of favorable outcomes}}{\text{total number of possible outcomes}}$$

The probability of any event occurring will always be a fraction or decimal between 0 and 1. It may also be expressed as a percent. The probability of an event not occurring is referred to as that event's **complement**. The sum of an event's probability and the probability of that event's complement will always be 1.

HELPFUL HINT
An event with 0 (or 0%) probability will never occur, and an event with a probability of 1 (or 100%) is certain to occur.

If events are **dependent events**, the probability of one occurring changes the probability of the other event occurring. If events are **independent events**, the probability of one occurring does not affect the probability of the other event occurring. Rolling a die multiple times is independent: getting one number does not change the probability of getting any particular number on the next roll.

The probability of two *independent events* occurring is the product of the two events' probabilities:

$$P(A \text{ and } B) = P(A) \times P(B)$$

SAMPLE QUESTION

23) In 2018 in the United States, 3.2 million teachers were employed by public schools, and 0.5 million teachers were employed by private schools. What is the probability that a US teacher selected at random works at a private school?

A. 5%

B. 14%

C. 16%

D. 72%

E. 86%

ALGEBRA

PROPERTIES

The algebraic properties describe basic rules related to addition, subtraction, multiplication, and division. The names of the properties will not be included on the test, but it's important to understand what the properties are and how they are used. Subtraction and division are neither commutative nor associative.

Table 3.4. Algebraic Properties

Property	Explanation	Example
Commutative property of addition	Changing the order of the addends does not change the result.	$4 + 8 = 8 + 4$
Commutative property of multiplication	Changing the order of the factors does not change the result.	$5 \times 9 = 9 \times 5$
Associative property of addition	Changing the grouping of the addends does not change the result.	$(2 + 6) + 4 = 2 + (6 + 4)$
Associative property of multiplication	Changing the grouping of the factors does not change the result.	$(3 \times 5) \times 4 = 3 \times (5 \times 4)$
Distributive property of multiplication over addition	A factor outside parentheses enclosing a sum can be distributed to the terms inside the parentheses.	$7(10 + 3) = 7(10) + 7(3)$

SAMPLE QUESTION

24) Which of the following statements is correct?
   A. $x(y)(z) = x(y)(x)(z)$
   B. $x(y)(z) = x(y) + x(z)$
   C. $x(y + z) = x(y) + x(z)$
   D. $x(y + z) = x(y) + z$
   E. $(y + z)x = y + zx$

ALGEBRAIC EXPRESSIONS

An **algebraic expression** is a mathematical phrase involving both numbers and **variables**, such as x or a, that represent unknown values. Variables can be multiplied by **coefficients**, which are numbers placed in front of the variable. In the expression $2x + 3$, x is the variable, and 2 is the coefficient. The number 3 is called a constant because its value cannot vary.

A **term** is a collection of coefficients and variables multiplied together, such as $5a$ or $21xy$. The terms of algebraic expressions are separated by plus and minus signs.

Expressions are evaluated by plugging in a given value for the variable. This process has two steps:

1.   Substitute—replace the variable with the value assigned to it.

2.   Simplify—work out the expression according to the order of operations.

> **What is the value of $3x^2 - 4x + 1$ when $x = 5$?**
> Replace x with 5.
> $3x^2 - 4x + 1$
> $3(5)^2 - 4(5) + 1 = 56$

To add or subtract algebraic expressions, combine like terms. Like terms have the same variable (or no variable) raised to the same power. Note that variables that stand alone have a coefficient of 1.

> **Simplify the expression: $(3x^2 - 4x + 2) - (x^2 + 2x + 5)$**
> Remove the parentheses, distributing –1 to the second expression.
> $(3x^2 - 4x + 2) - (x^2 + 2x + 5)$
> $= 3x^2 - 4x + 2 - x^2 - 2x - 5$
> Combine like terms.
> $= 3x^2 - x^2 - 4x - 2x + 2 - 5$
> $= 2x^2 - 6x - 3$

SAMPLE QUESTION

25) Which of the following is equivalent to $3x(x + 7) + 4x(2x - 6)$ for all values of x?

    A.   12
    B. $7x$
    C. $10x + 22$
    D. $11x^2 - 3x$
    E. $11x^2 - x + 1$

ALGEBRAIC EQUATIONS

An **equation** is a mathematical sentence that contains an equal sign: it states that two expressions are equal to each other. Because the two sides of the equation are equal, the same operation can be performed on both sides of the equation and it will still be true.

Solving an equation means finding the value of the variable that makes the equation true. This value can be found by performing operations so that the variable is alone on one side of the equal sign and a constant is on the other side of the equal sign.

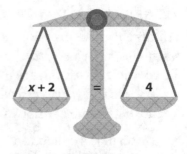

Figure 3.13. Equations

> **Solve for x: $4x + 5 = 2x - 7$**
> Subtract $2x$ from both sides.

$$4x + 5 = 2x - 7$$
$$4x - 2x + 5 = 2x - 2x - 7$$
$$2x + 5 = -7$$
Subtract 5 from both sides.
$$2x + 5 - 5 = -7 - 5$$
$$2x = -12$$
Divide both sides by 2.
$$\frac{2x}{2} = \frac{-12}{2}$$
$$x = -6$$

SAMPLE QUESTIONS

26) If $x + 15 = 4y$, and $y = 6$, what is the value of x?

A.   5

B.   6

C.   7

D.   8

E.   9

27) Which of the following statements are valid steps in solving the equation $3x + 9 = 24$? Select all correct answers.

[A] $12x = 24$

[B] $3x = 33$

[C] $3x = 15$

[D] $x = 2$

[E] $x = 5$

LINEAR RELATIONSHIPS

A **linear equation** has two variables, usually x and y. The solution to a linear equation isn't a single value but is instead two values called an **ordered pair**, written as (x, y). For example $(3,3)$ and $(-1,-5)$ are both solutions of the equation $y = 2x - 3$:

$(3,3)$: Plug in 3 for x and 3 for y.
$$y = 2x - 3$$
$$3 = 2(3) - 3$$
$$3 = 3$$

$(-1,-5)$: Plug in -1 for x and -5 for y.
$$y = 2x - 3$$
$$-5 = 2(-1) - 3$$
$$-5 = -5$$

Linear equations have an infinite number of solutions. These solutions can be graphed on the **coordinate plane**, which shows the *x*-value on the horizontal axis and the *y*-value on the vertical axis. Plotting all the solutions to a linear equation gives a straight line.

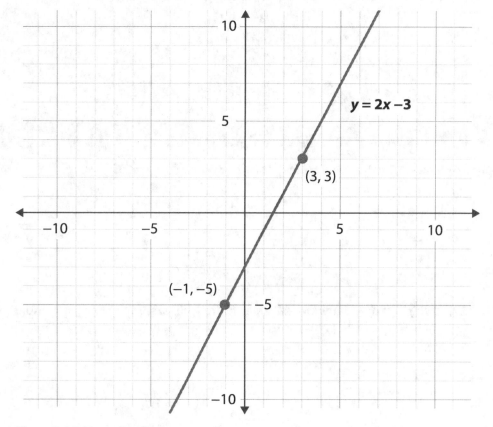

Figure 3.14. Linear Equation

Slope (*m*) is a number that describes the slant of a line on a coordinate plane. A line with a positive slope rises from left to right; a line with a negative slope falls from left to right. The greater the absolute value of a line's slope, the steeper it is.

To find the slope, choose two points on the graph, and count the difference in the *x*- and *y*-values. The slope will be the change in *y* divided by the change in *x*: $m = \frac{\text{change in } y}{\text{change in } x}$.

Another useful characteristic of a line is its **y-intercept** (*b*), the point at which the line crosses the *y*-axis. This point will always have the form (0, *b*).

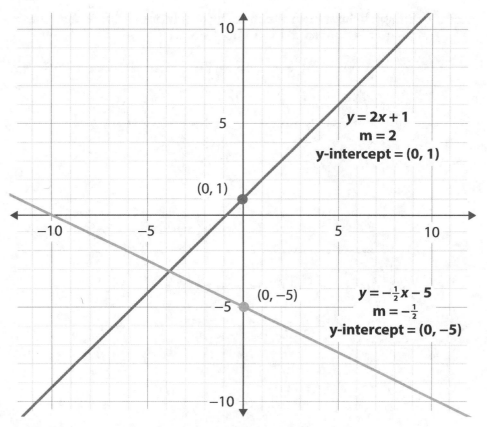

Figure 3.15. Slope and the y-Intercept in the Coordinate Plane

A linear equation in the form $y = mx + b$ is in **slope-intercept form** where m represents the slope of the line and b represents its y-intercept.

SAMPLE QUESTIONS

28) What is the slope of the line whose equation is $6x - 2y - 8 = 0$?

A. -4

B. $-\frac{2}{3}$

C. $\frac{1}{4}$

D. 3

E. 4

29) The graph below shows the shipping cost (*y*) for customers purchasing a number of textbooks (*x*) from a bookstore.

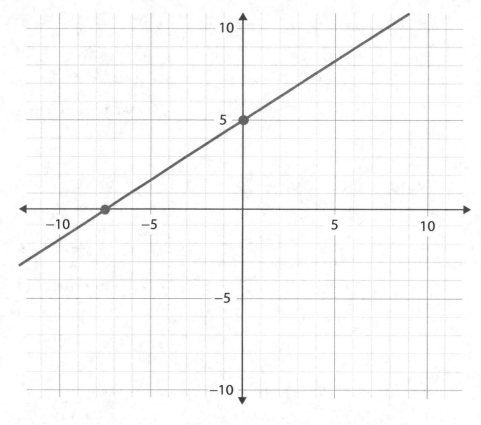

If a customer purchases 100 textbooks, how much will shipping cost?

WORD PROBLEMS

Mathematic expressions and equations can be used to model real-life situations. Often these situations are presented as **word problems** that can be translated from words into mathematical terms.

When working word problems, start by identifying the known and unknown values. Unknown values can be assigned a variable. Next, write an expression or equation that describes the mathematical relationship between those values. If necessary, the equation can then be solved.

Table 3.5 gives some common phrases and shows how they are translated into mathematical terms.

Table 3.5. Translating Word Problems

Words	Math Translation	Example
equals, is, will be, yields	=	x is the same as y x = y
add, increase, added to, sum, combined, more than	+	2 more than x x + 2
minus, decreased, less than, subtracted, took away, difference between	−	3 less than x x − 3
multiplied by, times, product of	×	the product of x and y x × y
divided by, per, out of	÷	x divided by y x ÷ y

SAMPLE QUESTIONS

30) **Joe's Rental Cars charges $35 plus 25 cents per mile to rent a car for one day. If Dan paid $90 to rent a car, how many miles did he drive?**

31) **Which problems below could be solved with the equation $12x + 15 = 195$? Select all correct answers.**

[A] Marissa has $15. She wants to buy a stereo that costs $195. How much will Marissa need to save each month to be able to buy the stereo in a year?

[B] Jason has $15 and plans to save $15 per week. How long will it take him to have $195?

[C] Dana has $15 and plans to save $12 per week. How long will it take her to have $195?

[D] Casey has $15 and plans to save $195 per month. How much money will she have in a year?

[E] Nate spends $12, and now he has $195. How much money did he have to begin with?

Geometry

Lines and Angles

Geometric figures are shapes composed of points, lines, or planes. A **point** is simply a location in space; it does not have any dimensional properties such as length, area, or volume. Points are written as a single capital letter, such as *A* or *Q*.

A collection of points that extends infinitely in both directions is a *line*, and one that extends infinitely in only one direction is a *ray*. A section of a line with a beginning and end is a *line segment*. A line segment is described by the beginning and end point, such as *AQ*. Lines, rays, and line segments are examples of **one-dimensional objects** because they can only be measured in one dimension (length).

Lines, rays, and line segments can intersect to create angles, which are measured in degrees or radians. Angles are classified based on the number of degrees they contain.

▶ Angles between 0 and 90 degrees are **acute**.

▶ Angles between 90 and 180 degrees are **obtuse**.

▶ An angle of exactly 90 degrees is a **right angle**.

Two angles with measurements that add up to 90 degrees are **complementary**, and two angles with measurements that add up to 180 degrees are **supplementary**. Two adjacent (touching) angles are called a **linear pair**, and they are supplementary.

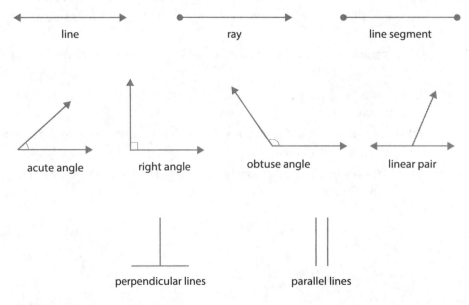

Figure 3.16. Lines and Angles

SAMPLE QUESTION

32) Mrs. Cortez is working with her students on comparing angles. A worksheet includes a picture of the following angle and asks students to draw a larger angle.

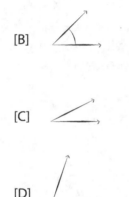

Which of the following student answers is correct? Select all correct answers .

[A]

[B]

[C]

[D]

PROPERTIES OF TWO-DIMENSIONAL SHAPES

Two-dimensional objects can be measured in two dimensions (length and width). A **plane** is a two-dimensional object that extends infinitely in both dimensions.

Polygons are two-dimensional shapes, such as triangles and squares, that have three or more straight sides. **Regular polygons** are polygons with sides that are all the same length.

> **HELPFUL HINT**
>
> Because all the points on a circle are equidistant from the center, all the circle's radii have the same length.

A **circle** is the set of all the points in a plane that are the same distance from a fixed point (called the **center**). The distance from the center to any point on the circle is the **radius** of the circle. The **diameter** is the largest measurement across a circle. It passes through the circle's center, extending from one side of the circle to the other. The measure of the diameter is twice the measure of the radius.

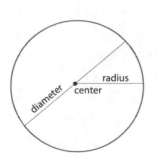

Figure 3.17. Parts of a Circle

Triangles have three sides and three interior angles that always sum to 180°. A **scalene triangle** has no equal sides or angles. An **isosceles triangle** has two equal sides and two equal angles (often called base angles). In an **equilateral triangle**, all three sides are equal as are all three angles. Moreover, because the sum of the angles of a triangle is always 180°, each angle of an equilateral triangle must be 60°.

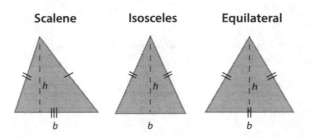

Figure 3.18. Types of Triangles

Quadrilaterals have four sides and four angles. In a **rectangle**, each of the four angles measures 90° and there are two pairs of sides with equal lengths. A square also has four 90° angles, and all four of its sides are an equal length.

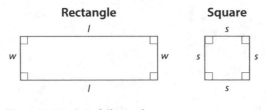

Figure 3.19. Quadrilaterals

The size of the surface of a two-dimensional object is its **area**. The distance around a two-dimensional figure is its **perimeter**, which can be found by adding the lengths of all the sides.

Table 3.6. Area and Perimeter of Basic Shapes			
Shape	**Area**	**Perimeter**	**Variables**
Triangle	$A = \frac{1}{2}bh$	$P = s^1 + s^2 + s^3$	b = base
			h = height
Square	$A = s^2$	$P = 4s$	s = side
			l = length
Rectangle	$A = l \times w$	$P = 2l + 2w$	w = width
			r = radius
Circle	$A = \pi r^2$	$C = 2\pi r$	C = circumference

SAMPLE QUESTIONS

33) Which of the following expressions describes the area of the triangle below?

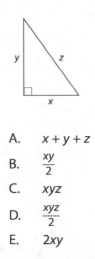

    A. $x + y + z$

    B. $\dfrac{xy}{2}$

    C. xyz

    D. $\dfrac{xyz}{2}$

    E. $2xy$

34) The figure below shows a square with four equal cutouts on each corner. What is the area of the resulting shape?

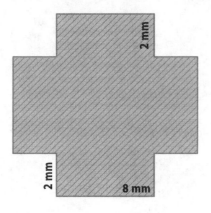

    A.   6 mm²

    B.   16 mm²

    C.   64 mm²

    D.   128 mm²

    E.   144 mm²

CONGRUENCY AND SIMILARITY

When discussing shapes in geometry, the term **congruent** is used to mean that two shapes have the same shape and size (but not necessarily the same orientation or location). For example, if the lengths of two lines are equal, the two lines themselves are called congruent. Congruence is written using the symbol $\cong$. On figures, congruent parts are denoted with hash marks. (See Figure 3.20.)

Shapes that are similar have the same shape but the not the same size, meaning their corresponding angles are the same but their lengths are not. For two shapes to be similar, the ratio of their corresponding sides must be a constant (called the scale factor). Similarity is described using the symbol ~.

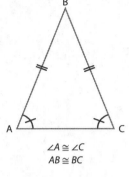

$\angle A \cong \angle C$
$AB \cong BC$

Figure 3.20. Congruent Parts of a Triangle

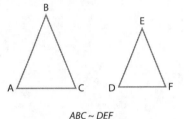

$ABC \sim DEF$

$$\frac{AB}{DE} = \frac{BC}{EF} = \frac{AC}{DF}$$

Figure 3.21. Similar Triangles

SAMPLE QUESTION

35) The figure below shows similar triangles ABC and DEF.

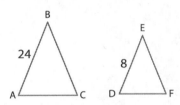

Which of the following statements is true?

A. $DF = \frac{AC}{3}$

B. $DF = AC - 16$

C. $DF = 2AC$

D. $DF = \frac{2}{3}AB$

E. $DF = AB - 8$

PROPERTIES OF THREE-DIMENSIONAL SHAPES

Three-dimensional objects, such as cubes, can be measured in three dimensions (length, width, height). Three-dimensional objects are also called **solids**, and the shape of a flattened solid is called a **net**.

The **surface area** (*SA*) of a three-dimensional object can be figured by adding the areas of all the sides. Surface area is measured in square units (e.g., m² or ft²). **Volume** (*V*) is the amount of space that a

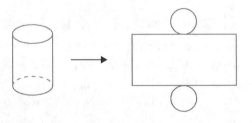

Figure 3.22. Net of a Cylinder

three-dimensional object takes up. Volume is measured in cubic units (e.g., ft^3 or mm^3).

A **rectangular solid** has six rectangular sides. A **cube** is a type of rectangular solid in which all the sides are squares. Every rectangular solid has a width (w), a length (l), and a height (h). Its surface area is the sum of the area of each rectangle, and its volume is found by multiplying the width, length, and height.

$$SA = 2lw + 2hw + 2hl$$
$$V = wlh$$

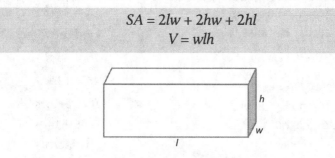

Figure 3.23. Rectangular Solid

SAMPLE QUESTION

36) A rectangular tank with a width of 3 meters and a length of 5 meters is filled with 30 cubic meters of water. What will be the height of the water in meters?

ANSWER KEY

1) A.   **Correct.** Integers include both positive and negative numbers, while whole numbers are always positive (except zero). The number −5 is an integer but not a whole number because it is negative.

2) B.   **Correct.** Because the temperature went down, add a negative number (or subtract).

$-3 + -5 = \mathbf{-8°F}$

3) C.   **Correct.** Multiply the number of boxes by the number of pencils in each box to find the total number of pencils.

$24 \times 110 = \mathbf{2640\ pencils}$

4) C.   **Correct.** $4^3 = 4 \times 4 \times 4 = 64$

5) C.   **Correct.** The square root of 100 is 10.

$10 \times 10 = 100$

6) C.   **Correct.** First , simplify the expression in parentheses.

$7 + 24 \div 8 \times \mathbf{(4-6)}^2 = 7 + 24 \div 8 \times (-2)^2$

Next, simplify the exponential expression.

$7 + 24 \div 8 \times \mathbf{(-2)^2} = 7 + 24 \div 8 \times 4$

Then, multiply and divide, working from left to right.

$7 + \mathbf{24 \div 8} \times 4 = 7 + 3 \times 4$

$7 + \mathbf{3 \times 4} = 7 + 12$

Finally, add: $7 + 12 = \mathbf{19}$

7) C.   **Correct.** Find the factors of 12.

$12 = 12 \times 1$

$12 = 6 \times 2$

$12 = 4 \times 3$

Find the factors of 26.

$26 = 26 \times 1$

$26 = 13 \times 2$

The factors of 12 are **1**, **2**, 3, 4, 6, and 12.

The factors of 26 are **1**, **2**, 13, and 26.

The shaded region will contain the numbers 1 and 2.

8) C.   **Correct.** 7 of 8 pizza slices are left after Carla takes 1, so $\frac{7}{8}$ of the pizza remains. **7** is the numerator of this fraction.

9) $\frac{\mathbf{3}}{\mathbf{20}}$

Find $\frac{1}{5}$ of $\frac{3}{4}$ by multiplying the fractions:

$\frac{1}{5} \times \frac{3}{4} = \frac{3}{20}$

10) D.   **Correct.** $1.3208 \div 5.2 = 0.2\underline{5}4$

The 5 is in the hundredths place.

11) A.   **Correct.** The 8 is in the thousands place. Because the value to the right of the 8 is less than 5, the 8 remains the same and all values to its right become zero. The result is **498,000**.

12) E.   **Correct.** Start by converting the fraction in the list to a decimal.

$\frac{1}{2} = 0.5$

The new list is now all decimals.

0.5, ___, 0.825

Now convert the other fractions to decimals.

$\frac{1}{3} = 0.33...$

$\frac{4}{5} = 0.8$

Find the decimal value that falls within 0.5 and 0.825.

$0.5 < \mathbf{0.8} < 0.825$

Choose the answer choice with the original fraction.

$\frac{1}{2}, \frac{4}{5}, 0.825$

13)   **3:2**

Find the number of women working at the company.

30 – 12 = 18 women

Write the ratio as the number of women over the number of men working at the company.

$\frac{\text{number of women}}{\text{number of men}} = \frac{18}{12}$

Reduce the ratio.

$\frac{18 \div 6}{12 \div 6} = \frac{3}{2}$

The ratio of women to men is $\frac{3}{2}$ or **3:2**.

14)   **B.**   **Correct.** Write a proportion using x for the missing value.

$\frac{60 \text{ kg}}{90 \text{ mg}} = \frac{80 \text{ kg}}{x}$

Cross-multiply and solve for x.

$60(x) = 80(90)$

$60x = 7200$

$x = 120$

The proper dosage is 120 mg.

15)   **20**

Set up a proportion and solve.

$\frac{\text{part}}{\text{whole}} = \frac{\%}{100}$

$\frac{16}{x} = \frac{80}{100}$

$16(100) = 80(x)$

$\mathbf{x = 20}$

16)   **A.**   **Correct.** Use the formula for percent change to find the sales price for each book.

amount of change = original amount × percent change

amount of change = $16 × 0.08 = $1.28

new price = $16 + $1.28 = $17.28

To find the store owner's profit, subtract the amount he paid for the books from the amount he made selling them.

$17.28(100) – $16(100) = **$128**

17)   **E.**   **Correct.** Most adults are between 1 and 2 meters tall. A kilometer and a mile are too large for measuring an adult's height. Pounds measure mass, and liters measure volume.

18)   **B.**   **Correct.** Use dimensional analysis.

$\frac{10,000 \text{ gal}}{\square} \times \frac{1 \text{ min}}{x \text{ gal}}$

$= \frac{\mathbf{10,000}}{\mathbf{x}}$ minutes

19)   **E.**   **Correct.** Even though the problem does not give the four individual scores, it can be assumed that each test

score was 81 (because four scores of 81 would average to 81). To find the score, x, that she needs:

$$\frac{4(81) + x}{5} = 83$$

$$324 + x = 415$$

$$x = 91$$

The student must score a 91 on the last test to have a mean score of 83.

20)   **346**

Range is the smallest value subtracted from the largest value.

$$418 - 72 = \mathbf{346}$$

21)   **C.**   **Correct.** The highest temperature is around 90°F, and the lowest temperature is around 60°F. Subtract to find the range.

$$90 - 60 = \mathbf{30}$$

22)   **B.**   **Correct.** Count the number of scores: there are 19 total values in the set.

Count from the top or bottom to find the middle (10th) value.

9	9, 8, 8, 5, 2, 1
8	8, 8, 8, **4**, 2
7	9, 8, 6, 2
6	7, 7, 3
5	5

$$9|9 = 99$$

23)   **B.**   **Correct.** Use the formula for probability.

$$P(\text{an event}) =$$

$$\frac{\text{number of favorable outcomes}}{\text{total number of possible outcomes}}$$

$$= \frac{\text{number of private school teachers}}{\text{total number of teachers}}$$

$$= \frac{500{,}000}{3{,}200{,}000 + 500{,}000} = 0.14$$

$$= \mathbf{14\%}$$

24)   **C.**   **Correct.** The expression in choice C applies the distributive property correctly by distributing the factor outside the parentheses to the terms inside the parentheses.

25)   **D.**   **Correct.** Apply the distributive property to each term.

$$3x(x + 7) = 3x^2 + 21x$$

$$4x(2x - 6) = 8x^2 - 24x$$

Combine like terms.

$$(3x^2 + 21x) + (8x^2 - 24x)$$

$$3x^2 + 8x^2 + 21x - 24x$$

$$= \mathbf{11x^2 - 3x}$$

26)   **E.**   **Correct.** Substitute $y = 6$ into the equation.

$$x + 15 = 4y$$

$$x + 15 = 4(6)$$

$$x + 15 = 24$$

Subtract 15 from both sides to solve for x.

$$x + 15 - 15 = 24 - 15$$

$$\mathbf{x = 9}$$

27)   **C. and E. are correct.**

Subtract 9 from both sides.

$$3x + 9 = 24$$

$$3x + 9 - 9 = 24 - 9$$

$$3x = 15$$

Divide both sides by 3.

$$\frac{3x}{3} = \frac{15}{3}$$

$$\mathbf{x = 5}$$

28) D. **Correct.** Rearrange the equation into slope-intercept form by solving the equation for *y*.

$6x - 2y - 8 = 0$

$-2y = -6x + 8$

$y = 3x - 4$

The slope is 3, since it is the coefficient of *x*.

29) **80**

Use the graph to find the equation that models shipping cost. The slope of the line is $\frac{3}{4}$ and the *y*-intercept is 5.

$y = \frac{3}{4}x + 5$

Plug $x = 100$ into the equation to find the shipping cost for 50 textbooks.

$y = \frac{3}{4}(100) + 5 = 75 + 5 = \$80$

30) **220**

Represent the unknown quantity with a variable.

m = number of miles

Write an equation to represent the facts in the problem. The rental company will multiply the number of miles by 25 cents and add the $35 base charge.

$0.25m + 35 = 90$

Solve the equation.

$0.25m = 55$

$m = 220$

Dan drove 220 miles.

31) **A. and C. are correct.** In choice A, *x* represents the amount of money Marissa will save each month. It is

multiplied by 12 (because there are 12 months in a year) and added to the $15 she had to begin with, for a total of $195.

In choice C, *x* represents the number of weeks that Dana will save money. It is multiplied by $12 per week and added to the $15 she had to begin with, for a total of **$195**.

32) A. Incorrect. This student tried to draw a larger angle by extending the rays farther from the vertex.

B. Incorrect. This student increased the size of the angle symbol but did not increase the size of the angle.

C. Incorrect. This student drew a smaller angle.

D. **Correct.** This student drew a larger angle.

33) B. **Correct.** The formula for the area of a triangle is $\frac{1}{2}bh$, where *b* is the base and *h* is the height. In this triangle, *y* is the base and *x* is the height, so the triangle's area is $\frac{1}{2}xy$, or $\frac{xy}{2}$.

34) D. **Correct.** Find the area of the square without the cutouts; each side would be 12 mm long.

$12 \text{ mm} \times 12 \text{ mm} = 144 \text{ mm}^2$

Next, find the area of the cutouts.

$2 \text{ mm} \times 2 \text{ mm} = 4 \text{ mm}^2$

$4 \times 4 \text{ mm}^2 = 16 \text{ mm}^2$

Finally, subtract the total area of the four cutouts from the total area of the square without the cutouts.

$144 - 16 = \mathbf{128 \ mm^2}$

35) **A.** **Correct.** Use the given lengths to find the scale ratio for the two triangles.

$\frac{AB}{DE} = \frac{24}{8} = 3$

The ratio of *DF* to *AC* will also be equal to 3 because they are corresponding parts of the two triangles.

$\frac{AC}{DF} = 3$

Solve for *DF*.

$\mathbf{DF = \frac{AC}{3}}$

36) **2**

Use the formula for the volume of a rectangular solid to solve for the height (*h*).

$V = wlh$

$30 \ m^3 = (3 \ m)(5 \ m)(h)$

$\mathbf{h = 2 \ meters}$

Practice Test

READING

Read the passage or graphic, and then answer the questions that follow.

Use the following passage for questions 1–5.

In recent decades, jazz has been associated with New Orleans and festivals like Mardi Gras, but in the 1920s, jazz was a booming trend whose influence reached into many aspects of American culture. In fact, the years between World War I and the Great Depression were known as the Jazz Age, a term coined by F. Scott Fitzgerald in his famous novel *The Great Gatsby*. Sometimes also called the Roaring Twenties, this time period saw major urban centers experiencing new economic, cultural, and artistic vitality. In the United States, musicians flocked to cities like New York and Chicago, which became famous hubs for jazz musicians. Ella Fitzgerald, for example, moved from Virginia to New York City to begin her much-lauded singing career, and jazz pioneer Louis Armstrong got his big break in Chicago.

Jazz music was played by and for a more expressive and freed populace than the United States had previously seen. Women gained the right to vote and were openly seen drinking and dancing to jazz music. This period marked the emergence of the flapper, a woman determined to make a statement about her new role in society. Jazz music also provided the soundtrack for the explosion of African American art and culture now known as the Harlem Renaissance. In addition to Fitzgerald and Armstrong, numerous musicians, including Duke Ellington, Fats Waller, and Bessie Smith, promoted their distinctive and complex music as an integral part of the emerging African American culture.

1

What is the main idea of the passage?

A.   People should associate jazz music with the 1920s, not modern New Orleans.

B.   Jazz music played an important role in many cultural movements of the 1920s.

C.   Many famous jazz musicians began their careers in New York City and Chicago.

D.   African Americans were instrumental in launching jazz into mainstream culture.

E.   The Jazz Age was a period of cultural and artistic exuberance, which had little economic or political significance.

2

The passage supports which of the following claims about jazz music?

A.   Jazz music was important to minority groups struggling for social equality in the 1920s.

B.   Duke Ellington, Fats Waller, and Bessie Smith were the most important jazz musicians of the Harlem Renaissance.

C.   Women gained the right to vote with the help of jazz musicians.

D.   Duke Ellington, Fats Waller, and Bessie Smith all supported women's right to vote.

E.   The success of jazz music contributed to a spike in America's economic wealth.

3

Which of the following is NOT a fact stated in the passage?

A.   The years between World War I and the Great Depression were known as the Jazz Age.

B.   Ella Fitzgerald and Louis Armstrong both moved to New York City to start their music careers.

C.   Women danced to jazz music during the 1920s to make a statement about their role in society.

D.   Jazz music was an integral part of the emerging African American culture of the 1920s.

E.   In modern-day popular culture, jazz music is most often associated with New Orleans and Mardi Gras.

4

The primary purpose of the passage is to

A.   explain the role jazz musicians played in the Harlem Renaissance.

B.   inform the reader about the many important musicians playing jazz in the 1920s.

C.   discuss how jazz influenced important cultural movements in the 1920s.

D.   provide a history of jazz music in the 20th century.

E.   describe how jazz music and the Roaring Twenties are depicted in modern-day popular culture.

5

Which conclusion about jazz music is supported by the passage?

A.   F. Scott Fitzgerald supported jazz musicians in New York and Chicago.

B.   Jazz music is no longer as popular as it once was.

C.   Both women and African Americans used jazz music as a way of expressing their newfound freedom.

D.   Flappers and African American musicians worked together to produce jazz music.

E.   Jazz music was a direct result of the economic wealth the country was experiencing at the time.

Use the following passage for question 6.

It has now been two decades since the introduction of thermonuclear fusion weapons into the military inventories of the great powers, and more than a decade since the United States, Great Britain, and the Soviet Union ceased to test nuclear weapons in the atmosphere. Today our understanding of the technology of thermonuclear weapons seems highly advanced, but our knowledge of the physical and biological consequences of nuclear war is continuously evolving.

6

The passage is primarily concerned with

A.   the impact of thermonuclear weapons on the military.

B.   the technology of thermonuclear weapons.

C.   atmospheric testing of nuclear weapons.

D.   the physical and biological consequences of nuclear war.

E.   the nuclear ceasefire between the United States, Great Britain, and the Soviet Union.

Use the following passage for question 7.

In Greek mythology, two gods, Epimetheus and Prometheus, were given the work of creating living things. Epimetheus gave good powers to the different animals. To the lion he gave strength; to the bird, swiftness; to the fox, sagacity; and so on. Eventually, all of the good gifts had been bestowed, and there was nothing left for humans. As a result, Prometheus returned to heaven and brought down fire, which he gave to humans. With fire, human beings could protect themselves by making weapons. Over time, humans developed civilization.

7

As used in the passage, "bestowed" most nearly means

A. purchased.

B. forgotten.

C. accepted.

D. given.

E. lost.

Use the following passage for questions 8–10.

It could be said that the great battle between the North and South we call the Civil War was a battle for individual identity. The states of the South had their own culture, one based on farming, independence, and the rights of both man and state to determine their own paths. Similarly, the North had forged its own identity as a center of centralized commerce and manufacturing. This clash of lifestyles was bound to create tension, and this tension was bound to lead to war. But people who try to sell you this narrative are wrong. The Civil War was not a battle of cultural identities—it was a battle about slavery. All other explanations for the war are either a direct consequence of the South's desire for wealth at the expense of her fellow man or a fanciful invention to cover up this sad portion of our nation's history. And it cannot be denied that this time in our past was very sad indeed.

8

The primary purpose of the passage is to

A. convince readers that slavery was the main cause of the Civil War.

B. illustrate the cultural differences between the North and the South before the Civil War.

C. persuade readers that the North deserved to win the Civil War.

D. demonstrate that the history of the Civil War is too complicated to be understood clearly.

E. describe the various causes of the American Civil War.

9

As used in the passage, "fanciful" most nearly means

A.   complicated.

B.   imaginative.

C.   successful.

D.   unfortunate.

E.   opulent.

10

What is the main idea of the passage?

A.   The Civil War was the result of cultural differences between the North and South.

B.   The Civil War was caused by the South's reliance on slave labor.

C.   The North's use of commerce and manufacturing allowed it to win the war.

D.   The South's belief in the rights of man and state cost the war.

E.   America's reliance on slave labor in the centuries before the Civil War is a sad and shameful part of the country's history.

Use the following passage for question 11.

After looking at five houses, Robert and I have decided to buy the one on Forest Road. The first two homes we visited didn't have the space we need—the first had only one bathroom, and the second did not have a guest bedroom. The third house, on Pine Street, had enough space inside but didn't have a big enough yard for our three dogs. The fourth house we looked at, on Rice Avenue, was stunning but well above our price range. The last home, on Forest Road, wasn't in the neighborhood we wanted to live in. However, it had the right amount of space for the right price.

11

What is the author's conclusion about the house on Pine Street?

A.   The house did not have enough bedrooms.

B.   The house did not have a big enough yard.

C.   The house was not in the right neighborhood.

D.   The house was too expensive.

E.   The house had the right amount of space for the right price.

Use the following passage for question 12.

For an adult to be unable to swim is criminal negligence: every man, woman, and child should learn. A person who cannot swim is a danger not only to himself but also to the people around him. Children as early as the age of four may acquire the art; no one is too young or too old.

12

Which of the following best captures the author's purpose?

A.   to encourage the reader to learn to swim

B.   to explain how people who cannot swim are a danger to others

C.   to inform the reader that it is never too late to learn to swim

D.   to argue that people who cannot swim should be punished

E.   to describe an effective way to teach swimming to adults

Use the following passage and graph for questions 13 and 14.

As you can see from the graph, my babysitting business has been really successful. The year started with a busy couple of months—several snows combined with a large number of requests for Valentine's Day services boosted our sales quite a bit. The spring months have admittedly been a bit slow, but we're hoping for a big summer once school gets out. Several clients have already put in requests for our services!

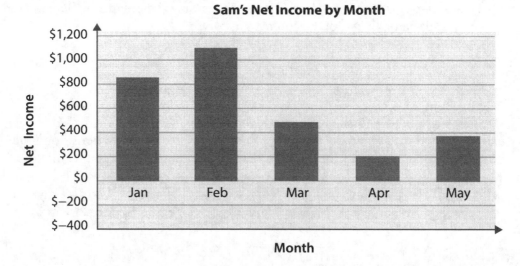

13

Based on the information in the graph, how much more did Sam's Babysitting Service bring in during February than during April?

A. $200

B. $900

C. $1,100

D. $1,300

E. $1,800

14

Which of the following best describes the tone of the passage?

A. professional

B. casual

C. concerned

D. neutral

E. disheartened

Use the following passage for questions 15–19.

Taking a person's temperature is one of the most basic and common health care tasks. Everyone from nurses to emergency medical technicians to concerned parents should be able to grab a thermometer to take a patient or loved one's temperature. But what's the best way to get an accurate reading? The answer depends on the situation.

The most common way people measure body temperature is orally. A simple digital or disposable thermometer is placed under the tongue for a few minutes, and the task is done. There are many situations, however, when measuring temperature orally isn't an option. For example, when a person can't breathe through the nose, they won't be able to keep their mouth closed long enough to get an accurate reading. In these situations, it's often preferable to place the thermometer in the rectum or armpit. Using the rectum also has the added benefit of providing a much more accurate reading than other locations can provide.

In addition, certain people, like agitated patients or fussy babies, won't be able to sit still long enough for an accurate reading. In these situations, it's best to use a thermometer that works much more quickly, such as one that measures temperature in the ear or at the temporal artery. No matter which method is chosen, however, it's important to check the average temperature for each region, as it can vary by several degrees.

15

Which statement is NOT a fact from the passage?

A. Taking a temperature in the ear or at the temporal artery is more accurate than taking it orally.

B. If an individual cannot breathe through the nose, taking their temperature orally will likely give an inaccurate reading.

C. The standard human body temperature varies depending on whether it's measured in the mouth, rectum, armpit, ear, or temporal artery.

D. The most common way to measure temperature is by placing a thermometer in the mouth.

E. Some patients are unable to sit still long enough for an accurate reading using an oral thermometer.

16

The primary purpose of the passage is to

A. advocate for the use of thermometers that measure temperature in the ear or at the temporal artery.

B. explain the methods available to measure a person's temperature and the situation where each method is appropriate.

C. warn readers that the average temperature of the human body varies by region.

D. discuss how nurses use different types of thermometers depending on the type of patient they are examining.

E. inform readers of the proper procedure for taking a baby's temperature.

17

Which of the following is the best summary of this passage?

A. It's important that everyone knows the best way to take a person's temperature in any given situation.

B. The most common method of taking a person's temperature—orally—isn't appropriate in some situations.

C. The most accurate way to take a temperature is placing a digital thermometer in the rectum.

D. There are many different ways to take a person's temperature, and which is appropriate will depend on the situation.

E. Nurses and parents must take special steps when taking the temperatures of fussy babies.

18

As used in the passage, "agitated" most nearly means

A. obviously upset.

B. quickly moving.

C. violently ill.

D. slightly dirty.

E. physically comfortable.

19

According to the passage, why is it sometimes preferable to take a person's temperature rectally?

A. Rectal readings are more accurate than oral readings.

B. Many people cannot sit still long enough to have their temperatures taken orally.

C. Temperature readings can vary widely between regions of the body.

D. Many people do not have access to quick-acting thermometers.

E. People who are ill may not be able to sit still long enough to have their temperatures taken through their ears or temporal arteries.

Use the following passage for question 20.

When the Spanish-American War broke out in 1898, the US Army was small and understaffed. President William McKinley called for 1,250 volunteers, primarily from the Southwest, to serve in the First US Volunteer Cavalry. Eager to fight, the ranks were quickly filled by a diverse group of cowboys, gold prospectors, hunters, gamblers, Native Americans, veterans, police officers, and college students looking for an adventure. The officer corps was composed of veterans of the Civil War and the Indian Wars. With more volunteers than it could accept, the army set high standards: all the recruits had to be skilled on horseback and with guns. Consequently, they became known as the Rough Riders.

20

According to the passage, all the recruits were required to

A.   have previously fought in a war.

B.   be American citizens.

C.   live in the Southwest.

D.   ride a horse well.

E.   have a college degree.

Use the following passage for questions 21–26.

Popcorn is often associated with fun and festivities, both in and out of the home. It's eaten in theaters, usually after being salted and smothered in butter, and in homes, fresh from the microwave. But popcorn isn't just for fun—it's also a multimillion-dollar-a-year industry with a long and fascinating history.

While popcorn might seem like a modern invention, its history actually dates back thousands of years, making it one of the oldest snack foods enjoyed around the world. Popcorn is believed by food historians to be one of the earliest uses of cultivated corn. In 1948, Herbert Dick and Earle Smith discovered old popcorn dating back 4,000 years in the New Mexico Bat Cave. For the Aztec Indians who called the caves home, popcorn (or *momochitl*) played an important role in society, both as a food staple and in ceremonies. The Aztecs cooked popcorn by heating sand in a fire; when it was heated, kernels were added and would pop when exposed to the heat of the sand.

The American love affair with popcorn began in 1912, when popcorn was first sold in theaters. The popcorn industry flourished during the Great Depression when it was advertised as a wholesome and economical food. Selling for five to ten cents a bag, it was a luxury that the downtrodden could afford. With the introduction of mobile popcorn machines at the World's Columbian Exposition, popcorn moved from the theater into fairs and parks. Popcorn continued to rule the snack food kingdom until the rise in popularity of home televisions during the 1950s.

The popcorn industry reacted to the decline in sales quickly by introducing pre-popped and unpopped popcorn for home consumption. However, it wasn't until microwave popcorn became commercially available in 1981 that at-home popcorn consumption began to grow exponentially. With the wide availability of microwaves in the United States, popcorn also began popping up in offices and hotel rooms. However, the home still remains the most popular popcorn eating spot: today, 70 percent of the 16 billion quarts of popcorn consumed annually in the United States are eaten at home.

21

The passage supports which of the following claims about popcorn?

A.   People ate less popcorn in the 1950s than in previous decades because they went to the movies less.

B.   Without mobile popcorn machines, people would not have been able to eat popcorn during the Great Depression.

C.   People enjoyed popcorn during the Great Depression because it was a luxury food.

D.   During the 1800s, people began abandoning theaters to go to fairs and festivals.

E.   Today, popcorn is a popular snack food because of its wholesomeness and affordability.

22

As used in the passage, "staple" most nearly means

A.   something produced only for special occasions.

B.   something produced regularly in large quantities.

C.   something produced by cooking.

D.   something fastened together securely.

E.   something of high nutritional value.

23

What is the best summary of this passage?

A.   Popcorn is a popular snack food that dates back thousands of years. Its popularity in the United States has been tied to the growth of theaters and the availability of microwaves.

B.   Popcorn has been a popular snack food for thousands of years. Archaeologists have found evidence that many ancient cultures used popcorn as a food staple and in ceremonies.

C.   Popcorn was first introduced to America in 1912, and its popularity has grown exponentially since then. Today, over 16 billion quarts of popcorn are consumed in the United States annually.

D.   Popcorn is a versatile snack food that can be eaten with butter or other toppings. It can also be cooked in a number of different ways, including in microwaves.

E.   Popcorn is a versatile snack food that can be enjoyed in any number of locations such as theaters, festivals, at home, and even at work.

24

The primary purpose of the passage is to

A.   explain how microwaves affected the popcorn industry.

B.   show that popcorn is older than many people realize.

C.   illustrate the history of popcorn from ancient cultures to modern times.

D.   demonstrate the importance of popcorn in various cultures.

E.   highlight the large increase in profits that the popcorn industry has seen in recent decades.

25

Which factor does the author of the passage credit for the growth of the popcorn industry in the United States?

A.   the use of popcorn in ancient Aztec ceremonies

B.   the growth of the home television industry

C.   the marketing of popcorn during the Great Depression

D.   the nutritional value of popcorn

E.   the introduction of pre-popped and unpopped popcorn to the market

26

Which of the following is NOT a fact stated in the passage?

A.   Archaeologists have found popcorn dating back 4,000 years.

B.   Popcorn was first sold in theaters in 1912.

C.   Consumption of popcorn dropped in 1981 with the growing popularity of home televisions.

D.   Seventy percent of the popcorn consumed in the United States is eaten in homes.

E.   The popcorn industry flourished during the Great Depression.

Use the following passage for question 27.

The Scream of Nature by Edvard Munch is one of the world's best known and most desirable artworks. While most people think of it as a single painting, the iconic creation actually has four different versions: two paintings and two pastels. In 2012, one of the pastels earned the fourth highest price paid for a painting at auction when it was sold for almost $120 million. The three others are not for sale; the Munch Museum in Oslo holds a painted version and a pastel version, while the National Gallery in Oslo holds the other painting. However, the desire to acquire them has been just as strong: in 1994 the National Gallery's version was stolen, and in 2004 the painting at the Munch Museum was stolen at gunpoint in the middle of the day. Both paintings were eventually recovered.

27

The primary purpose of the passage is to

A. describe the image depicted in *The Scream in Nature*.

B. explain the origin of the painting *The Scream in Nature*.

C. clarify the number of versions of *The Scream in Nature* that exist.

D. prove the high value of *The Scream in Nature*.

E. outline the different ownerships of *The Scream in Nature*.

Use the following passage for questions 28–30.

In its most basic form, geography is the study of space; more specifically, it studies the physical space of the earth and the ways in which it interacts with, shapes, and is shaped by its habitants. Geographers look at the world from a spatial perspective. This means that at the center of all geographic study is the question, *where?* For geographers, the *where* of any interaction, event, or development is a crucial element to understanding it.

This question of *where* can be asked in a variety of fields of study, so there are many subdisciplines of geography. These can be organized into four main categories: (1) regional studies, which examine the characteristics of a particular place; (2) topical studies, which look at a single physical or human feature that impacts the whole world; (3) physical studies, which focus on the physical features of Earth; and (4) human studies, which examine the relationship between human activity and the environment.

28

A researcher studying the relationship between farming and river systems would be engaged in which of the following geographical subdisciplines?

A. regional studies

B. topical studies

C. physical studies

D. human studies

E. physical and human studies

29

Which of the following best describes the mode of the passage?

A. expository

B. narrative

C. persuasive

D. descriptive

E. rhetorical

30

Which of the following is a concise summary of the passage?

A. The most important questions in geography are where an event or development took place.

B. Geography, which is the study of the physical space on Earth, can be broken down into four subdisciplines.

C. Regional studies is the study of a single region or area.

D. Geography can be broken down into four subdisciplines: regional studies, topical studies, physical studies, and human studies.

E. The relationship between humans and their physical space is an important one.

Use the following passage for question 31.

After World War I, powerful political and social forces pushed for a return to normalcy in the United States. The result was disengagement from the larger world and increased focus on American economic growth and personal enjoyment. Caught in the middle of this was a cache of American writers, raised on the values of the prewar world and frustrated with what they viewed as the superficiality and materialism of postwar American culture. Many of them, like Ernest Hemingway and F. Scott Fitzgerald, fled to Paris, where they became known as the "lost generation," creating a trove of literary works criticizing their home culture and delving into their own feelings of alienation.

31

In the third sentence, the word "cache" most nearly means

A. a group of the same type.

B. a majority segment.

C. an organization.

D. a dispersed number.

E. a new school.

Use the following passages for questions 32–40.

Passage One

In the field of veterinary medicine, the inquiry into whether animals experience pain the same way humans do is especially important in the context of pain management. Although many advancements have been made in research sciences and pain management is widely accepted as a necessary job of practitioners, a number of myths about animal pain still plague the field of veterinary medicine and prevent practitioners from making pain management a priority. According to veterinarian and writer Debbie Grant, three myths are especially detrimental to the cause.

The first is the myth that animals do not feel pain at all or that they feel it less intensely than humans; in fact, according to Grant, the biological mechanisms by which we experience pain are the very same mechanisms by which animals experience pain. Even the emotional reaction to a painful experience, like being afraid to return to the dentist after an unpleasant visit, is mirrored in animals.

The second myth that prevents the advancement of pain management practices is the myth that pain is a necessary part of an animal's recovery. While some veterinarians believe that pain may prevent a healing dog, for example, from playing too vigorously, Grant says this is simply not the case. In fact, restlessness and discomfort may even lead to unusually high levels of agitation and may consequently slow the recovery process even further.

Finally, contrary to the third myth, animals do not necessarily tolerate pain any better than humans do, though they may handle their pain differently. Grant emphasizes that veterinarians must be aware that a lack of obvious signs does not necessarily suggest that pain is not present: in fact, many animals are likely to conceal their pain out of an instinct to hide weaknesses that may make them easy targets for predators.

Passage Two

Unlike doctors, who typically have the benefit of discussing their patients' concerns, veterinarians cannot ask their patients whether and where they are experiencing discomfort. Additionally, veterinarians must be aware of the survival instinct of many animals to mask pain in response to the foreign environment of a veterinary office. For these reasons, diagnostic tools and strategies are instrumental in the effective practice of veterinary medicine.

Veterinarians have a unique challenge when it comes to diagnosing their patients. In 2014, researchers of veterinary medicine at the University of Perugia in Italy completed a review of the diagnostic tools and strategies available to today's practitioners and found a number of them to be effective. Presumptive diagnosis, the first of these strategies, involves making a prediction about the animal's pain based on the observable damage to the body or body part. In addition to presumptive diagnosis, veterinarians can use close observation to assess changes in the animal's behavior.

The most common tool for performing diagnosis is the clinical exam, which can include both a physical exam and laboratory testing. As part of this process, a veterinarian might make use of an objective pain scale, by which he or she could assess the animal's condition according to a number of criteria. This tool is especially useful throughout the course of treatment, as it provides the practitioner with a quantitative measure for evaluating the effectiveness of various treatment options.

32

As it is used in Passage One, the term "detrimental" most nearly means

A. mischievous.

B. damaging.

C. disturbing.

D. advantageous.

E. confusing.

33

The author of Passage One most likely includes the example of the unpleasant dentist visit in order to

A.   provide a relatable example of how pain can influence a person's emotions.

B.   challenge the reader to overcome his or her natural, emotional response to painful experiences.

C.   question a popular perception about the experience of going to the dentist.

D.   highlight a similarity in the way humans and animals respond to pain.

E.   remind the reader of how scary the dentist is for children.

34

The author of Passage One indicates that despite advancements in veterinary sciences, many veterinarians

A.   do not see the value in pain management practices for their patients.

B.   still employ outdated methods of pain management.

C.   still believe that pain management is a responsibility of the pet owner.

D.   still have misguided beliefs and practices related to pain management in animals.

E.   do not have the technology to provide effective pain management options.

35

The author of Passage Two indicates that veterinarians can improve their pain management practices by

A.   attempting to communicate with their patients about the pain they are experiencing.

B.   employing the best diagnostic practices in their field.

C.   encouraging pet owners to keep careful watch over their animals.

D.   inventing novel ways to assess and treat pain in animals.

E.   focusing on the causes of the pain rather than pain itself.

36

The author of Passage Two indicates that objective pain measures are useful because

A.   they allow the veterinarian to compare an animal's pain level to the pain levels of other animals.

B.   they challenge the veterinarian to devise a treatment plan as quickly as possible.

C.   they discount the assumption that pain cannot be measured on an objective scale.

D.   they provide the veterinarian with a quantitative method for tracking pain levels over the course of an animal's treatment.

E.   they offer a new perspective on the management of pain in small animals.

37

The author of Passage 1 would most likely respond to the discussion of presumptive diagnosis in Passage 2 by

A. asserting that substantial physical damage to an animal's form does not necessarily suggest the presence of pain.

B. asserting that presumptive diagnosis is more effective for diagnosing humans and should not be used for diagnosing animals.

C. asserting that similarities in methods of pain diagnosis for humans and animals are effective because of the biological similarities between them.

D. asserting that veterinarians should not make use of presumptive diagnosis in evaluating and treating patients.

E. asserting that the pain diagnosis is much more difficult in humans than in animals.

38

Which of the following best describes the relationship between the two passages?

A. The first passage makes the claim that pain management should be a priority for veterinarians, while the second passage rejects this claim.

B. The first passage emphasizes the veterinarian's responsibility to prioritize pain management in animals, while the second passage explores the tools by which veterinarians can execute this responsibility.

C. The first passage seeks to dispel myths about pain management in animals, while the second passage denies that they are myths.

D. The first passage sheds light on the shortcomings of veterinary sciences as they currently exist, while the second passage provides insight into how these shortcomings might be overcome.

E. The first passage describes early approaches to pain management in animals, while the second passage highlights more modern approaches.

39

Both authors indicate that veterinarians

A. must be aware that a lack of obvious symptoms does not necessarily suggest an absence of pain.

B. should make pain management for their patients a priority.

C. ought to be familiar with the misguided assumptions that exist in their field.

D. need to conduct a thorough examination before releasing an animal back to its owner.

E. should prioritize oral health care in order to prevent the need for painful procedures.

40

As it is used in Passage Two, the term "foreign" most nearly means

A.   unfamiliar.

B.   inaccessible.

C.   distant.

D.   exotic.

E.   dangerous.

Use the following graph for question 41.

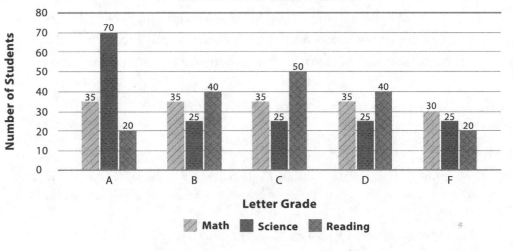

END-OF-YEAR GRADE REPORT

41

Which conclusion can be drawn from the graph?

A.   More than twice as many students earned an A in science than earned an F in science.

B.   The majority of students earned a C in math.

C.   The number of students who earned a B in reading is equal to the number of students who earned a B in math.

D.   Next year's students will not need intensive science instruction.

E.   More students earned a C in science than earned a D in science.

Use the following passage for question 42.

One of the most dramatic acts of nonviolent resistance in India's movement for independence from Britain came in 1930, when independence leader Mahatma Gandhi organized a 240-mile march to the Arabian Sea. The goal of the march was to make salt from seawater, in defiance of British law. The British prohibited Indians from collecting or selling salt—a vital part of the Indian diet—requiring them instead to buy it from British merchants and pay a heavy salt tax. The crowd of marchers grew along the way to tens of thousands of people. In Dandi, Gandhi picked up a small chunk of salt and broke British law. Thousands in Dandi followed his lead as did millions of fellow protestors in coastal towns throughout India. In an attempt to quell the civil disobedience, authorities arrested more than 60,000 people across the country, including Gandhi himself.

42

With which of the following claims about civil disobedience would the author most likely agree?

A.   Civil disobedience is a disorganized form of protest easily quashed by government.

B.   Civil disobedience requires extreme violations of existing law to be effective.

C.   Civil disobedience is an effective strategy for effecting political change.

D.   Civil disobedience is only effective in countries that already have democracy.

E.   Civil disobedience can only work on a small scale to effect local change.

Use the following passage for questions 43–45.

Vexillology, the study of flags, became its own field of study in the mid-twentieth century. Who studies flags? Historians, sociologists, designers, and those simply interested in these ubiquitous signals. Flags are everywhere: homeowners fly them from their houses, balconies, or poles on lawns. Government buildings display them prominently.

Many people first think of flags that represent nationality. But there are other types of flags, too. For instance, coastal authorities may display flags at the beach indicating conditions for swimming and boating. Similarly, various flags are used by boaters to communicate on the high seas. Sports fans may wave the flags of their favorite teams at the game or display these flags at their homes. Still, most flags are indeed associated with a country, and there are over two hundred countries and territories on Earth today.

With so many different flags, it makes sense that the International Federation of Vexillogical Associations (which uses the acronym FIAV, reflecting its French name) meets to organize flag study and safeguard flag history. According to the FIAV, vexillology became an organized field in response to the decolonization and revolutionary movements of the 1960s, when many countries became independent for the first time. There was a need to keep track of new flags, so volunteers stepped up and the organization grew. Today, FIAV comprises several national associations of vexillology and meets regularly to discuss topics of interest.

43

As used in the passage, "prominently" most nearly means

A.   occasionally.

B.   visibly.

C.   rarely.

D.   outside.

E.   fashionably.

44

What is the main idea of this passage?

A.   It is important to study flags because countries use them.

B.   Vexillology and flags are controlled by one major group: the FIAV.

C.   The FIAV helps keep track of the many types of flags in the world today.

D.   Flags are only used to identify countries.

E.   The United Nations decides which countries may use which flags.

45

The reader can infer that "there was a need to keep track of new flags" following the decolonization period of the 1960s because

A.   many countries became independent around the same time and adopted national flags, causing a need for organization to avoid duplicates and other problems.

B.   due to the instability during the era of decolonization and revolutions, countries were at war over many issues, including flag design.

C.   an international organization was needed to grant flags to the many new countries that had gained independence.

D.   a number of new flags were issued to enhance communication on the high seas, now that more independent countries existed.

E.   more people became interested in vexillology during this time.

Use the following passage for question 46.

When a fire destroyed San Francisco's American Indian Center in October of 1969, American Indian groups set their sights on the recently closed island prison of Alcatraz as a site of a new Indian cultural center and school. Ignored by the government, an activist group known as Indians of All Tribes sailed to Alcatraz in the early morning hours with eighty-nine men, women, and children. They landed on Alcatraz, claiming it for all the tribes of North America. Their demands were ignored, so the group continued to occupy the island for the next nineteen months, its numbers swelling up to six hundred as others joined. By January of 1970, many of the original protestors had left, and on June 11, 1971, federal marshals forcibly removed the last residents.

46

The main idea of this passage is that

A.   the government refused to listen to the demands of American Indians.

B.   American Indians occupied Alcatraz in protest of government policy.

C.   few people joined the occupation of Alcatraz, weakening its effectiveness.

D.   the government took violent action against protestors at Alcatraz.

E.   American Indians wanted Alcatraz to be a new cultural center.

Use the following passage for question 47.

Increasingly, companies are turning to subcontracting services rather than hiring full-time employees. This provides companies with many advantages like greater flexibility, reduced legal responsibility to employees, and lower possibility of unionization within the company. However, it has also led to increasing confusion and uncertainty over the legal definition of employment. Recently, the courts have grappled with questions about the hiring company's responsibility in maintaining fair labor practices. Companies argue that they delegate that authority to the subcontractors, while unions and other worker advocate groups argue that companies still have a legal obligation to the workers who contribute to their business.

47

The primary purpose of the passage is to

A.   critique the labor practices of modern companies.

B.   explain why companies prefer subcontracting work.

C.   highlight a debate within the business and labor community.

D.   describe a recent court decision related to labor practices.

E.   provide evidence for the benefits of subcontracting to workers.

Use the following passage for questions 48 – 53.

The bacteria, fungi, insects, plants, and animals that live together in a habitat have evolved to share a pool of limited resources. They've competed for water, minerals, nutrients, sunlight, and space—sometimes for thousands or even millions of years. As these communities have evolved, the species in them have developed complex, long-term interspecies interactions known as symbiotic relationships.

Ecologists characterize these interactions based on whether each party benefits. In mutualism, both individuals benefit, while in synnecrosis, both organisms are harmed. A relationship where one individual benefits and the other is harmed is known as parasitism. Examples of these relationships can easily be seen in any ecosystem. Pollination, for example, is mutualistic—pollinators get nutrients from the flower, and the plant is able to reproduce—while tapeworms, which steal nutrients from their host, are parasitic.

There's yet another class of symbiosis that is controversial among scientists. As it's long been defined, commensalism is a relationship where one species benefits and the other is unaffected. But is it possible for two species to interact and for one to remain completely unaffected? Often, relationships described as commensal include one species that feeds on another species' leftovers; remoras, for instance, will attach themselves to sharks and eat the food particles they leave behind. It might seem like the shark gets nothing from the relationship, but a closer look will show that sharks in fact benefit from remoras, which clean the sharks' skin and remove parasites. In fact, many scientists claim that relationships currently described as commensal are just mutualistic or parasitic in ways that haven't been discovered yet.

48

The primary purpose of the passage is to

A.   argue that commensalism isn't actually found in nature.

B.   describe the many types of symbiotic relationships.

C.   explain how competition for resources results in long-term interspecies relationships.

D.   provide examples of the many different ways individual organisms interact.

E.   explain the differences between commensalism and mutualism.

49

Which of the following is NOT a fact stated in the passage?

A.   Mutualism is an interspecies relationship where both species benefit.

B.   Synnecrosis is an interspecies relationship where both species are harmed.

C.   The relationship between plants and pollinators is mutualistic.

D.   The relationship between remoras and sharks is parasitic.

E.   Commensalism is a topic of controversy in the scientific community.

50

Epiphytes are plants that attach themselves to trees and derive nutrients from the air and surrounding debris. Sometimes, the weight of epiphytes can damage the trees on which they're growing. The relationship between epiphytes and their hosts would be described as

A.   mutualism.

B.   commensalism.

C.   parasitism.

D.   synnecrosis.

E.   atypical.

51

As used in the passage, "controversial" most nearly means

A. debatable.

B. objectionable.

C. confusing.

D. upsetting.

E. offensive.

52

According to the passage, why is commensalism controversial among scientists?

A. Many scientists believe that an interspecies interaction where one species is unaffected does not exist.

B. Some scientists believe that relationships where one species feeds on the leftovers of another should be classified as parasitism.

C. Because remoras and sharks have a mutualistic relationship, no interactions should be classified as commensalism.

D. Only relationships among animal species should be classified as commensalism.

E. Some scientists believe animals are incapable of interspecies interaction.

53

Which conclusion about symbiotic relationships is supported by the passage?

A. Scientists cannot decide how to classify symbiotic relationships among species.

B. The majority of interspecies interactions are parasitic because most species do not get along.

C. If two species are involved in a parasitic relationship, one of the species will eventually become extinct.

D. Symbiotic relationships evolve as the species that live in a community adapt to their environments and each other.

E. Mutualistic relationships are rare and difficult to maintain.

Use the following passage for question 54.

In 1989, almost a million Chinese university students descended on central Beijing, protesting for increased democracy and calling for the resignation of Communist Party leaders. For three weeks, they marched, chanted, and held daily vigils in the city's Tiananmen Square. The protests had widespread support in China, particularly among factory workers who cheered them on. For Westerners watching, it seemed to be the beginning of a political revolution in China, so the world was stunned when, on July 4, Chinese troops and security police stormed the square, firing into the crowd. Chaos erupted with some students trying to fight back by throwing stones and setting fire to military vehicles. Tens of thousands more attempted to flee. While official numbers were never given, observers estimated anywhere from 300 to thousands of people were killed, while 10,000 were arrested.

54

It can be inferred from the passage that after July 4

A. the protest movement in China gained increasing support.

B. Western countries intervened on behalf of the university protestors.

C. factory workers took action in defense of the protestors.

D. the government implemented significant reforms to military practices.

E. the movement for increased democracy in China fell apart.

Use the following passage for questions 55 and 56.

At midnight on Saturday, August 12, 1961, units of the East German army moved into position and began closing the border between East and West Berlin. Destroying streets that ran parallel to the border to make them impassable, they installed ninety-seven miles of barbed wire and fences around West Berlin and another twenty-seven miles along the border between West and East Berlin. By Sunday morning the border was completely shut down. Families woke up that morning suddenly divided, and some East Berliners with jobs in the west were unable to get to work. West Berlin was now an isolated island surrounded by a communist government hostile to its existence. Thus began the most troubling period in German history.

55

The primary purpose of the passage is to

A. describe the impact of the closing of the Berlin border.

B. analyze East Germany's motives for closing the Berlin border.

C. explain the Western response to the closing of the Berlin border.

D. inform the reader about the methods used to close the Berlin border.

E. provide a history of the Berlin border.

56

Which of the following statements is an opinion?

A. Families woke up that morning suddenly divided.

B. Thus began the most troubling period in German history.

C. East Germany destroyed streets to make them impassable.

D. West Berlin was now an isolated island.

E. By Sunday morning the border was completely shut down.

WRITING

USAGE

Each question consists of a sentence with underlined portions. Determine if any of the underlined parts contain inappropriate word use, poor or incorrect grammatical construction, or incorrect or omitted punctuation or capitalization that needs revision to produce a correct sentence. If there are no errors in the sentence as written, select "No error." No sentence has more than one error.

1

Ukrainians (A)<u>celebrate</u> a holiday called Malanka during which men (B)<u>dress in</u> costumes and masks and (C)<u>plays</u> tricks on (D)<u>their</u> neighbors. (E)<u>No error</u>

2

As juveniles (A)<u>,</u> (B)<u>african</u> white-backed vultures are (C)<u>darkly</u> colored, developing their white feathers only as they (D)<u>grow into</u> adulthood. (E)<u>No error</u>

3

(A)<u>Because of</u> (B)<u>its</u> distance from the sun, the planet Neptune (C)<u>has seasons</u> that last the (D)<u>equivalent</u> of forty-one Earth years. (E)<u>No error</u>

4

Edward Jenner, (A)<u>considered</u> the father of immunology, invented the (B)<u>world's</u> first vaccine (C)<u>over infecting</u> a young boy with cowpox, successfully protecting him from the widespread (D)<u>,</u> and far more dangerous, smallpox virus. (E)<u>No error</u>

5

Everyday items like potatoes, (A)<u>bread,</u> onions, and even saliva (B)<u>is</u> the tools of art conservators, (C)<u>who</u> work to (D)<u>clean and restore</u> works of art. (E)<u>No error</u>

6

The Akhal-Teke horse breed, originally (A)<u>from</u> Turkmenistan, (B)<u>have</u> long enjoyed (C)<u>a reputation</u> for (D)<u>bravery and fortitude.</u> (E)<u>No error</u>

7

The employer (A)<u>decided</u> that he could not, (B)<u>due to</u> the high cost of health care, afford (C)<u>to offer</u> (D)<u>no other</u> benefits to his employees. (E)<u>No error</u>

8

Though Puerto Rico is known popularly for (A)<u>its</u> beaches, its landscape also (B)<u>includes</u> mountains, which (C)<u>are</u> home to many of the (D)<u>island's</u> rural villages. (E)<u>No error</u>

9

The photographer (A)<u>,</u> specializes in shooting portraits and taking still lifes, but she also (B)<u>likes</u> (C)<u>to accept</u> more challenging assignments, such as (D) <u>photographing</u> wildlife. (E)<u>No error</u>

10

In the fight (A)<u>against</u> obesity, (B)<u>countries'</u> around the world (C)<u>are</u> imposing taxes on sodas and other sugary drinks (D)<u>in hopes of</u> curbing unhealthy habits. (E)<u>No error</u>

11

The (A)<u>Black Death</u>, often thought of as a concern of times past, (B)<u>continued</u> to spread among rodent populations even today (C)<u>,</u> occasionally making (D)<u>its</u> way into a human host. (E)<u>No error</u>

12

Advances (A)<u>in</u> agricultural technology over the past five decades (B)<u>have led</u> to a steady increase in the global food (C)<u>supply, and</u> the (D)<u>population</u> of many countries around the world are benefiting. (E)<u>No error</u>

SENTENCE CORRECTION

In each of the following sentences, some part or all of the sentence is underlined. You are provided with five ways of writing the underlined part. The first choice is always the same as the original; the other four choices differ. Choose the answer that most effectively expresses the meaning of the sentence, while following the requirements of standard written English.

13

The famously high death toll at the end of the Civil War was not exclusively due to battle losses; <u>in addition,</u> large numbers of soldiers and civilians fell ill and died as a result of living conditions during the war.

A.   in addition,

B.   therefore,

C.   however,

D.   consequently,

E.   on the other hand,

14

The public defense attorney was able to maintain her optimism despite <u>her dearth of courtroom wins, lack of free time she had, and growing list of clients she was helping.</u>

A.   her dearth of courtroom wins, lack of free time she had, and growing list of clients she was helping.

B.   her dearth of courtroom wins, lack of free time, and how many clients she was helping.

C.   her dearth of courtroom wins, lack of free time, and growing list of clients.

D.   her dearth of courtroom wins, the free time she lacked, and the list of clients she was growing.

E.   the losses she had experienced, the free time she lacked, and her growing client list.

15

<u>Being invented in France in the early nineteenth century,</u> the stethoscope underwent a number of reiterations before the modern form of the instrument was introduced in the 1850s.

A.   Being invented in France in the early nineteenth century,

B.   Inventing in France in the early nineteenth century,

C.   It was invented in France in the early nineteenth century,

D.   Though it was invented in France in the nineteenth century,

E.   Invented in France in the early nineteenth century,

16

In 1983, almost twenty years after his death, T.S. Eliot won two Tony Awards for his contributions to the well-loved musical *Cats*, <u>it was based on a book of his poetry.</u>

A.   it was based on a book of his poetry.

B.   which was based on a book of his poetry.

C.   because it was based on a book of his poetry.

D.   being based on a book of his poetry.

E.   having been based on a book of his poetry.

17

Because the distance between stars in the galaxy is far greater than the distance between planets, interstellar travel <u>is expected to be an even bigger challenge than</u> interplanetary exploration.

A.   is expected to be an even bigger challenge than

B.   will be expected to be an even bigger challenge than

C.   is expected to be an even bigger challenge then

D.   is expecting to be an even bigger challenge than

E.   expects to be an even bigger challenge than

18

The <u>painters who are often confused for each other</u> Claude Monet and Édouard Manet actually did have a couple things in common: they were born only six years apart in Paris, France, and both contributed important early Impressionist works to the artistic canon.

A. painters who are often confused for each other

B. painters whose names are similar and who are sometimes confused as a result

C. common confused painters

D. painters who are confusing because of their similar names

E. commonly confused painters

19

The field of child development is concerned with <u>the emotional, the psychological, and biological development</u> of infants and children.

A. the emotional, the psychological, and biological development

B. the emotional, psychological, and biological development

C. the emotional development, the psychological, and the biological development

D. emotional, psychological, and the biological development

E. the emotional, psychological, and the biological development

20

Though it is often thought of as an extreme sport, spelunking involves much more than adrenaline: enthusiasts dive into unexplored caves <u>to study structures of, take photographs, and create maps of</u> the untouched systems.

A. to study structures of, take photographs, and create maps of

B. to study structures of, to take photographs, and create maps of

C. to study structures of, taking photographs of, and creating maps of

D. to study structures, take photographs, and create maps of

E. studying structures of, taking photographs, and creating maps of

21

In many European countries such as France, Spain, and Italy, <u>hot chocolate was made with real melted chocolate,</u> making for a beverage that is thick and rich.

A. hot chocolate was made with real melted chocolate,

B. hot chocolate had been made with real melted chocolate,

C. hot chocolate has been made with real melted chocolate

D. hot chocolate will be made with real melted chocolate,

E. hot chocolate is made with real melted chocolate,

22

Parrots, among the most intelligent birds in the world, have been prized pets for many <u>centuries, in fact, the first recorded instance of parrot training was written in the thirteenth century.</u>

A.   centuries, in fact, the first recorded instance of parrot training was written in the thirteenth century.

B.   centuries, but the first recorded instance of parrot training was written in the thirteenth century.

C.   centuries, writing the first recorded instance of parrot training in the thirteenth century.

D.   centuries, so the first recorded instance of parrot training was written in the thirteenth century.

E.   centuries; in fact, the first recorded instance of parrot training was written in the thirteenth century.

23

Engineers <u>designed</u> seat belts to stop the inertia of traveling bodies by applying an opposing force on the driver and passengers during a collision.

A.   designed

B.   are designing

C.   design

D.   were designing

E.   will have designed

24

The artist Prince, whose death shocked America in April 2016, was one of the most successful musical artists ever, <u>ranking twenty-seventh</u> on *Rolling Stone*'s 2010 list of "100 Greatest Artists of All Time."

A.   ranking twenty-seventh

B.   ranked twenty-seventh

C.   he ranked twenty-seventh

D.   he was ranking twenty-seventh

E.   he was ranked twenty-seventh

REVISION IN CONTEXT

PASSAGE ONE

The following passage is a draft of an essay that needs strengthening through editing and revision. Read the passage and choose the best answers for the questions that follow. Some questions will ask you to improve sentences or parts of sentences. Sometimes the portion in question may require no changes at all. Consider organization, development, tone, style, word choice, and the requirements of standard written English in answering the questions.

(1) For centuries, <u>artists and philosophers have long debated about the relationship between life and art.</u> (2) While some argue that art is an imitation of life, others believe that, just as often, life ends up imitating art. (3) In no other genre is the impact of art on our real lives more visible than in the realm of science fiction. (4) Great minds of science fiction such as Jules Verne, Gene Roddenberry, H. G. Wells, and Stanley Kubrick have introduced ideas that, though fantastical at the time of their inception, eventually became reality. (5) Many of these artists were dead before they ever saw their ideas come to life.

(6) Some of humanity's biggest accomplishments were achieved first in science fiction. (7) Jules Verne wrote about humanity traveling to the moon over a century before it happened. (8) Scientists Robert H. Goddard and Leo Szilard both credit his work—on liquid-fueled rockets and atomic power, respectively—to H. G. Wells and his futuristic novels. (9) Gene Roddenberry, the creator of *Star Trek*, dreamed up replicators long before 3-D printers were invented.

(10) Jules Verne's work, for example, was the inspiration for both the submarine and the modern-day helicopter. (11) H. G. Wells wrote about automatic doors long before they began to turn up in almost every grocery store in America. (12) Roddenberry's *Star Trek* is even credited as the inspiration for the creation of the mobile phone. (13) Kubrick's HAL from *2001: A Space Odyssey* represented voice control at its finest, long before virtual assistants were installed in all the new smartphone models.

25

In context, which revision to sentence 5 (reproduced below) is most needed?

Many of these artists were dead before they ever saw their ideas come to life.

A.   delete the sentence

B.   change *many* to *most*

C.   change *dead* to *deceased*

D.   change *saw* to *witnessed*

E.   change *their* to *they're*.

26

In context, which is the best version of the underlined portion of sentence 1 (reproduced below)?

artists and philosophers have long debated about the relationship between life and art.

A. artists and philosophers have examined the facts and debated about the relationship between life and art.

B. artists and philosophers have hemmed, hawed, and debated about the relationship between life and art.

C. artists and philosophers have debated about the relationship between life and art.

D. artists and philosophers have hemmed and hawed about the relationship between life and art.

E. artists and philosophers have forever and always debated about the relationship between life and art.

27

Which of the following introductory phrases should be inserted at the beginning of sentence 6 (reproduced below)?

Some of humanity's biggest accomplishments were achieved first in science fiction.

A. Therefore,

B. In fact,

C. However,

D. In addition,

E. Consequently,

28

In context, which revision to sentence 8 (reproduced below) is most needed?

Scientists Robert H. Goddard and Leo Szilard both credit his work—on liquid-fueled rockets and atomic power, respectively—to H. G. Wells and his futuristic novels.

A. delete the sentence

B. insert *always* after the word *both*

C. change *his* to *their*

D. delete the phrase inside the dashes

E. change *futuristic* to *future*

29

In context, which of the following would provide the best introduction to the final paragraph?

A. Transportation was of particular concern to science fiction writers, who dreamed up new ways for humanity to get around the world.

B. These same authors had other interesting ideas as well.

C. Sometimes science fiction is so much like life it is incredible.

D. Many of the ideas life borrows from science fiction have infiltrated our everyday lives and our world to an even greater degree.

E. Unfortunately, some of the dreams of these science fiction writers were more realistic than others.

30

In context, which of the following would provide the best conclusion to the essay?

A. Science fiction will, no doubt, continue to influence our technology and our world for many years to come.

B. These men are important figures in history for their ideas, and they should be respected as such.

C. Many other times, the ideas that turn up in science fiction never make it to the design table.

D. It is unfair that these creative individuals did not receive any money or rewards in exchange for their ideas.

E. Science fiction is really an interesting topic, with many ideas and influential people to study and understand.

Passage Two

The following passage is a draft of an essay that needs strengthening through editing and revision. Read the passage and choose the best answers for the questions that follow. Some questions will ask you to improve sentences or parts of sentences. Sometimes the portion in question may require no changes at all. Consider organization, development, tone, style, word choice, and the requirements of standard written English in answering the questions.

(1) Since its birth, humanity has sought explanations for the unexplainable. (2) In ancient cultures, mythology explained the weather, the elements of nature, and even the creation of the universe. (3) More recently, as recently as the last two centuries, many cultures have turned to folklore and superstition to explain odd occurrences and behaviors. (4) In the folk traditions of European countries, <u>one creature in particular takes the blame when individuals, especially children, begin acting strangely, the changeling.</u>

(5) According to many folk traditions, <u>changelings were the children of fairies or elves, left in the places of human children who had been stolen from their families by the creatures.</u> (6) If an individual's family began to notice strange behaviors in the individual, they would assume he or she had been kidnapped and replaced with a changeling. (7) This provided, at least, some answers to families whose children suffered from unexplained ailments or disabilities.

(8) Many families believed there were specific actions that would encourage the changeling to leave and return the human child. (9) In Germany, Ireland, and Wales, for example, it was thought that brewing egg shells would surprise the changeling into admitting his or her true identity. (10) Unfortunately, however, the belief that changelings could be convinced to leave was not just <u>an innocuous superstition.</u> <u>(11) On some occasions,</u> harm came to the individual who was thought to be a changeling.

31

Which of the following is the best way to introduce sentence 3 (reproduced below)?

More recently, as recently as the last two centuries, many cultures have turned to folklore and superstition to explain odd occurrences and behaviors.

A.   More recently,

B.   These days,

C.   Therefore,

D.   On the other hand,

E.   In addition,

32

Which is the best revision for the underlined portion of sentence 4 (reproduced below)?

one creature in particular takes the blame when individuals, especially children, begin acting strangely, the changeling.

A.   as it is now

B.   one creature in particular takes the blame when individuals, especially children, begin acting strangely: the changeling.

C.   one creature in particular takes the blame when individuals—especially children, begin acting strangely—the changeling.

D.   one creature in particular takes the blame when individuals especially children begin acting strangely. The changeling.

E.   one creature in particular takes the blame, when individuals, especially children, begin acting strangely—the changeling.

33

Which of the following would NOT be an acceptable revision of the underlined portion of sentence 5 (reproduced below)?

changelings were the children of fairies or elves, left in the places of human children who had been stolen from their families by the creatures.

A. changelings were the children of fairies or elves, who were left in the places of human children who had been stolen from their families by the creatures.

B. changelings were the children of fairies or elves; they were left in the places of human children who had been stolen from their families by the creatures.

C. changelings were the children of fairies or elves, they were left in the places of human children who had been stolen from their families by the creatures.

D. changelings were the children of fairies or elves—left in the places of human children who had been stolen from their families by the creatures.

E. changelings were the children of fairies or elves. These creatures were left in the places of human children who had been stolen from their families by the creatures.

34

Which revision to sentence 7 (reproduced below) is most needed?

This provided, at least, some answers to families whose children suffered from unexplained ailments or disabilities.

A. delete the sentence

B. insert *explanation* after *this* and before *provided*

C. change *families* to *family's*

D. change *whose* to *who's*

E. change *ailments* to *illnesses*

35

What is the best placement for sentence 8 (reproduced below)?

Many families believed there were specific actions that would encourage the changeling to leave and return the human child.

A. where it is now

B. at the end of the second paragraph

C. after sentence 9

D. after sentence 10

E. after sentence 11

36

Which is the best way to revise and combine sentences 10 and 11 (reproduced below) at the underlined point?

Unfortunately, however, the belief that changelings could be convinced to leave was not just <u>an innocuous superstition. On some occasions,</u> harm came to the individual who was thought to be a changeling.

A.   an innocuous superstition, on some occasions,

B.   an innocuous superstition, so on some occasions,

C.   an innocuous superstition, but on some occasions,

D.   an innocuous superstition; however, on some occasions,

E.   an innocuous superstition: on some occasions,

RESEARCH SKILLS

The following questions test your familiarity with basic research skills. For each question, choose the best answer.

37

Which of the following style guides would be appropriate for a student who was writing a research paper about the effects of rewards on human behavior?

A.   APA Style

B.   MLA Style

C.   Chicago Style

D.   The student should choose his or her preferred style.

E.   No style guide is required for this type of project.

38

Which of the following is an example of a primary source document?

A.   an essay that reviews the findings of a handful of related studies, compiled by an expert in the field

B.   a condemning article about the government's response in the aftermath of a tragedy, written by a young journalist who conducted interviews and read eyewitness accounts

C.   a critical review of a recently released novel, written by a renowned literature critic

D.   a paper discussing the results of an original study, conducted by the author

E.   a summary of a famous speech, composed by a political science professor

39

Which of the following could be incorporated into a research paper as a secondary source?

A. an interpretive essay about a famous piece of art, written by a well-respected art historian

B. the court transcript of a high-profile murder trial, compiled by a court stenographer

C. the journal entries of a student who witnessed a protest that turned riotous when police became involved

D. a video recording of the aftermath of a natural disaster, shot by a resident of the featured neighborhood

E. an audio recording of a politician admitting to wrongdoing, captured by a staff member

40

Harun is writing an essay about the migration patterns of birds. Which of the following facts would NOT be relevant to his research?

A. Within a species, the tendency to migrate might vary by the location of each population, as populations in areas that are warm year-round may not need to migrate in pursuit of food.

B. Only a small percentage of bird species actually migrate long distances, but some do complete shorter migratory journeys.

C. Of the species of bird that migrate, not all do so by flying: some bird species, such as the penguin, migrate in other ways, like by swimming.

D. Prior to the late eighteenth century, many people believed that birds hibernated during the winter; only later did they accept migration as an explanation for the absence of birds during winter.

E. Migration patterns may vary within a bird species based on age and gender.

ARGUMENTATIVE ESSAY

Discuss whether you agree or disagree with this opinion, and support your views with specific examples from your own observations, reading, or experience.

PROMPT

It has been said that a "mob mentality" takes over when people gather in a crowd, and otherwise law-abiding people behave inappropriately or worse. History is full of such examples, including riots and wars. It is impossible for a large group of people to remain rational and thoughtful when confronted with an emotional situation.

Source-Based Essay

You will have 30 minutes to read two short passages on a topic and then plan and write an informative essay on that topic based on the sources provided.

Passage One

Since the hugely successful launch of Paris's Velib public bicycle share program (PBSP) in 2007, PBSPs have become a worldwide movement. Over 100 programs operate in more than 150 cities around the world, including almost fifty US cities, providing alternative transportation to millions of people. However in cities like Seattle, Washington, and Melbourne, Australia, mandatory helmet laws designed to reduce injuries among bikers are stunting the growth of the system. While bikes in London and New York are typically used three to six times a day, those in Melbourne are used once at most. In 2016, Seattle's city council had to intervene when its bike program reached an unsustainably low level of participation. Even though the programs in these cities attempt to facilitate helmet access through specialized vending machines and even the availability of free helmets, mandatory helmet usage is a hurdle that deters most casual riders: the target market of PBSPs. PBSPs are a vital component of modern cities: they decrease congestion, diversify transportation options, and provide a low-cost transportation alternative for both tourists and residents. These benefits greatly outweigh the potential risk of increased injury from lack of helmet use.

Passage Two

The negative impact of mandatory helmet laws on public bicycle share programs is indisputable. However, programs that operate without such regulations pose significant public health risks. Public bicycle share systems target the casual rider who is less likely to own or carry a helmet. In systems in which helmets are available but not required, helmet usage is extremely low. Concentrated in urban areas with heavy traffic patterns, these programs encourage relatively inexperienced riders to ride in challenging conditions with insufficient protection. A study conducted by the National Institutes of Health found that in cities with public bicycle share systems, head injuries increased from 42.3 percent of bicycle-related injuries before implementation of the program to 50.1 percent after implementation, and that the proportion of bicycle-related head injuries that led to admission to a trauma center increased by 14 percent. Research since the first introduction of mandatory helmet laws in the 1990s shows a consistent decrease in bicycle-related traumatic brain injuries, ranging from a decrease of 45 to 75 percent. While fewer people may use the public bikes if a mandatory helmet law in place, it is a small price to pay to ensure the safety of those who do.

MATHEMATICS

Work the problem and then choose the most correct answer.

1

What is the greatest common factor of 45 and 22?

A.   0
B.   1
C.   2
D.   9
E.   11

2

The population of a town was 7250 in 2014 and 7375 in 2015. What was the percent increase from 2014 to 2015 to the nearest tenth of a percent?

A.   1.5%
B.   1.6%
C.   1.7%
D.   1.8%
E.   2.0%

3

Which of the following numbers are equivalent to 2.61? Indicate <u>all</u> such numbers.

[A]   2.610

[B] $\frac{261}{10}$

[C]   2.061

[D] $\frac{261}{100}$

[E] $\frac{261}{1000}$

4

Which number has the greatest value?

A.   9299 ones
B.   903 tens
C.   93 hundreds
D.   9 thousands
E.   9 thousandths

5

If a car uses 8 gallons of gas to travel 650 miles, how many miles can it travel using 12 gallons of gas?

A.   870 miles $\frac{650}{8}$ and multiply by 12
B.   895 miles
C.   915 miles
D.   975 miles
E.   1025 miles

6

The line of best fit is calculated for a data set that tracks the number of miles that passenger cars traveled annually in the US from 1960 to 2010. In the model, $x = 0$ represents the year 1960, and y is the number of miles traveled in billions. If the line of best fit is $y = 0.0293x + 0.563$, approximately how many additional miles were traveled for every 5 years that passed?

A.   0.0293 billion
B.   0.1465 billion
C.   0.5630 billion
D.   0.7100 billion
E.   2.9615 billion

7

The graph below shows the number of months that Chicago, New York, and Houston had less than 3 inches of rain from 2009 to 2015.

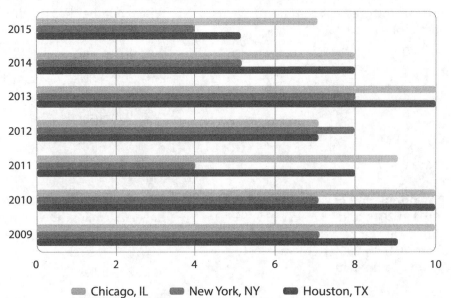

Number of Months with Less Than 3 Inches of Rain

Chicago, IL   New York, NY   Houston, TX

From 2009 to 2015, what is the average number of months that Chicago had less than 3 inches of rain?

A.   5

B.   6

C.   7

D.   8

E.   9

8

Rectangular water tank A is 5 feet long, 10 feet wide, and 4 feet tall. Rectangular tank B is 5 feet long, 5 feet wide, and 4 feet tall. If the same amount of water is poured into both tanks and the height of the water in tank A is 1 foot, how high will the water be in tank B?

A.   1 foot

B.   2 feet

C.   3 feet

D.   4 feet

E.   5 feet

9

In the sequence below, each term is found by finding the difference between the previous two numbers and multiplying the result by −3. What is the 6th term of the sequence?

{3, 0, 9, −27, ... }

A   −405

B.   −135

C.   45

D.   81

E.   135

10

Justine bought 6 yards of fabric to make some curtains, but she only used $4\frac{5}{8}$ yards. What fraction of the original fabric does she have left?

11

> If $a + b$ is an even number, then both a and b must be even.

Which of the following statements is a counterexample to the statement above?

A. $2 + 3 = 5$

B. $6 + 9 = 15$

C. $7 + 3 = 10$

D. $10 + 14 = 24$

E. $17 + 15 = 32$

12

The figure below shows a rectangle with 4 square cutouts made to each corner. What is the area of the resulting shape?

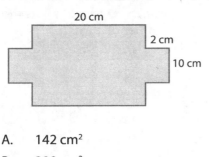

A.   142 cm²

B.   200 cm²

C.   296 cm²

D.   320 cm²

E.   492 cm²

13

Which expression below is equivalent to $10x + 4$? Select all that are equivalent.

[A] $4 + 10x$

[B] $2(8x + 7) - 5$

[C] $2(5x + 2)$

[D] $7x + 10 - 3x - 6$

[E] $6x + 7 + 4x - 3$

14

The ratio of nurses to doctors in a hospital unit is 3:1. Which of the following could be the total number of nurses and doctors in the unit?

A.   28

B.   30

C.   31

D.   34

E.   38

15

A group of 20 friends is planning a road trip. They have 3 cars that seat 4 people, 3 cars that seat 5 people, and 1 car that seats 6 people. What is the fewest number of cars they can take on the trip if each person needs his or her own seat?

A.   3 cars

B.   4 cars

C.   5 cars

D.   6 cars

E.   7 cars

16

Solve the following equation for *y*:
3(2*y* + 1) + 3 = 4(*y* – 2)

A.   –7

B.   –6

C.   –1

D.   7

E.   14

17

If a student answers 129 out of 150 questions correctly on a quiz, what percentage of questions did she answer incorrectly?

A.   10%

B.   12%

C.   14%

D.   15%

E.   17%

18

Solve the following equation for *x*:
6*x* – 7 = 5(2*x* + 1)

A.   –3

B.   –2

C.   3

D.   4

E.   5

19

The formula for distance is *d* = *v* × *t*, where *v* is the object's velocity and *t* is the time. How long will it take a plane to fly 4000 miles from Chicago to London if the plane flies at a constant rate of 500 mph?

A.   0.125 hours

B.   3.5 hours

C.   8 hours

D.   20 hours

E.   45 hours

20

A semicircle is drawn next to the base of an isosceles triangle such that its diameter is perpendicular to the triangle's altitude. What is the area of the resulting figure shown below?

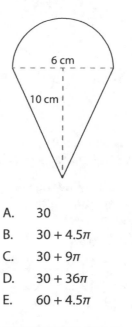

A.   30

B.   30 + 4.5π

C.   30 + 9π

D.   30 + 36π

E.   60 + 4.5π

21

Justin has a summer lawn care business and earns $40 for each lawn he mows. He also pays $35 per week in business expenses. Which of the following expressions represents Justin's profit after *x* weeks if he mows *m* number of lawns?

A.   40*m* – 35*x*

B.   40*m* + 35*x*

C.   35*x*(40 + *m*)

D.   35(40*m* + *x*)

E.   40*x*(35 + *m*)

22

An ice chest contains 24 sodas, some regular and some diet. The ratio of diet soda to regular soda is 1:3. How many regular sodas are there in the ice chest?

A.   1

B.   4

C.   6

D.   18

E.   24

23

At the grocery store, apples cost $1.89 per pound and oranges cost $2.19 per pound. How much would it cost to purchase 2 pounds of apples and 1.5 pounds of oranges?

A. $6.62

B. $7.07

C. $7.14

D. $7.22

E. $7.67

24

> 30, 27, 24, 21, . . .

Which of the following sequences follows the same rule as the sequence above?

A.   41, 39, 37, 35 , . . .

B.   41, 44, 47, 50, . . .

C.   41, 37, 33, 29, . . .

D.   41, 38, 35, 32, . . .

E.   41, 27, 24, 21, . . .

25

A car traveled at 65 miles per hour for $1\frac{1}{2}$ hours and then traveled at 50 miles per hour for $2\frac{1}{2}$ hours. How many miles did the car travel?

26

If $4x = 3$, what is the value of $8x$?

A.   0.75

B.   6

C.   12

D.   24

E.   32

27

Which of the angles in the figure below are congruent?

A. w and z

B. x and z

C. w and x

D. y and x

E. y and w

28

Which of the following is the y-intercept of the line whose equation is $7y - 42x + 7 = 0$?

A. $(\frac{1}{6}, 0)$

B. $(6, 0)$

C. $(0, -1)$

D. $(-1, 0)$

E. $(0, 6)$

29

Allison used $2\frac{1}{2}$ cups of flour to make a cake and $\frac{3}{4}$ of a cup of flour to make a pie. If she started with 4 cups of flour, how many cups of flour does she have left?

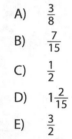

30

$\frac{4}{5} - \frac{1}{3} =$

A) $\frac{3}{8}$

B) $\frac{7}{15}$

C) $\frac{1}{2}$

D) $1\frac{2}{15}$

E) $\frac{3}{2}$

31

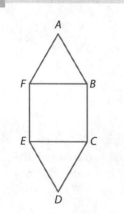

In the figure above, triangles ABF and CDE are equilateral. If the perimeter of the figure is 60 inches, what is the area of square BCEF in square inches?

A.   60

B.   100

C.   120

D.   140

E.   144

32

Points W, X, Y, and Z lie on a circle with center A. If the diameter of the circle is 75, what is the sum of AW, AX, AY, and AZ?

A.   75

B.   100

C.   125

D.   300

E.   150

33

Adam is painting the outside of a four-walled shed. The shed is 5 feet wide, 4 feet deep, and 7 feet high. How many square feet of paint will Adam need to paint the four sides of the shed?

A.   80

B.   126

C.   140

D.   252

E.   560

34

If the volume of a cube is 343 cubic meters, what is the cube's surface area?

A.   49 m²

B.   84 m²

C.   196 m²

D.   294 m²

E.   343 m²

35

The mean of 13 numbers is 30. If the mean of 8 of these numbers is 42, what is the mean of the other 5 numbers?

A.   5.5

B.   10.8

C.   16.4

D.   21.2

E.   30.0

36

Kendrick has $2386.52 in his checking account. If he pays $792.00 for rent, $84.63 for groceries, and $112.15 for his car insurance, how much money will he have left in his account?

A. $1397.74

B. $1482.37

C. $1509.89

D. $2189.22

E. $3375.30

37

In the fall, 425 students pass the math benchmark. In the spring, 680 students pass the same benchmark. What is the percentage increase in passing scores from fall to spring?

A.   37.5%

B.   55%

C.   60%

D.   62.5%

E.   80%

38

If one serving of milk contains 280 milligrams of calcium, how much calcium is in 1.5 servings?

A.   187 mg

B.   200 mg

C.   295 mg

D.   420 mg

E.   560 mg

39

Which of the following operations is equivalent to dividing by 100?

A.   multiplying by $\frac{1}{100}$

B.   adding −100

C.   dividing by $\frac{1}{100}$

D.   subtracting 100

E.   multiplying by 0.001

40

If $5x + 2 = 2y$ and $y = 6$, what is the value of x?

A.   2

B.   3

C.   4

D.   5

E.   6

41

Which of the following is equivalent to the term $5n$ for all values of n? Select all equivalent statements.

[A] $5n^5 - n^4$

[B] $3n + 2n$

[C] n^5

[D] $5 + n$

[E] $n + n + n + n + n$

42

Which of the following are factors of 790? Select all factors.

[A]   2

[B]   3

[C]   5

[D]   6

[E]   10

43

What number is in the hundredths place when 21.563 is divided by 8?

A.   3

B.   5

C.   6

D.   7

E.   9

44

A fifth-grade teacher has her class check a rain gauge every day for five days. The students then draw their data on a graph as shown below.

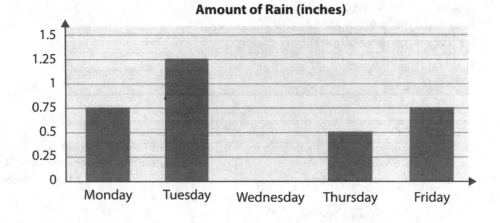

Amount of Rain (inches)

What was the average daily rainfall over the five days?

_____

45

Which of the following numbers is between $5\frac{1}{4}$ and $5\frac{1}{2}$?

A. $5\frac{5}{8}$

B. $5\frac{7}{20}$

C. $5\frac{3}{4}$

D. $5\frac{1}{10}$

E. $5\frac{8}{15}$

46

What is the median of all the even integers greater than 10 and less than 25?

A.   12

B.   14

C.   16

D.   18

E.   20

47

A 10 L container will hold how much more liquid than a 2 gallon container? (1 gal = 3.785 L)

A.   2.00 L

B.   2.43 L

C.   6.22 L

D.   8.00 L

E.   9.47 L

48

A cyclist is moving down the sidewalk at 15 feet per second. What is his approximate speed in miles per hour?

A.   10.2 mph

B.   15.9 mph

C.   17.1 mph

D.   22 mph

E.   30.7 mph

49

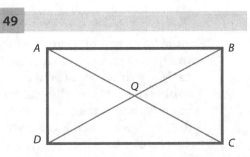

If *ABCD* is a rectangle, which of the following statements must be true?

A. ∠*AQD* ≅ ∠*AQB*

B. *AB* ≅ *AD*

C. △*AQD* ≅ △*BQC*

D. m∠*AQB* = 90°

E. *AB* = 2(*AD*)

50

In the Venn diagram below, set A includes all the factors of 24, and set B includes all the factors of 28. What is the probability that a number selected at random from the shaded region will be 2?

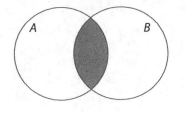

A. $\frac{1}{4}$

B. $\frac{1}{3}$

C. $\frac{1}{2}$

D. $\frac{2}{3}$

E. $\frac{3}{4}$

51

A restaurant employs servers, hosts, and managers in a ratio of 9:2:1. If there are 36 total employees, what is the number of hosts at the restaurant?

_____

52

Melissa is ordering fencing to enclose a square area of 5625 square feet. Which of the following is the number of feet of fencing she needs?

A. 75

B. 150

C. 300

D. 1405

E. 5625

53

A circular swimming pool has a circumference of 50 feet. Which of the following is the diameter of the pool in feet?

A) 25π

B) $\frac{25}{\pi}$

C) 50π

D) $\frac{50}{\pi}$

E) 50π + 25

54

The perimeter of a rectangle is 42 millimeters. If the length of the rectangle is 13 millimeters, what is its width in millimeters?

_____

55

The pie graph below shows how a state's government plans to spend its annual budget of $3 billion. How much more money does the state plan to spend on infrastructure than education?

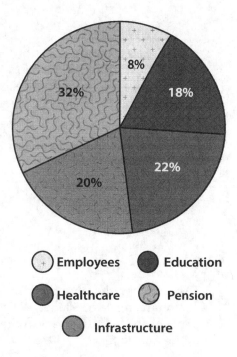

- Employees
- Education
- Healthcare
- Pension
- Infrastructure

A. $60,000,000
B. $120,000,000
C. $300,000,000
D. $540,000,000
E. $600,000,000

56

Robbie has a bag of treats that contains 5 pieces of gum, 7 pieces of taffy, and 8 pieces of chocolate. If Robbie reaches into the bag and randomly pulls out a treat, what is the probability that Robbie will get a piece of taffy?

A. $\frac{1}{13}$

B. $\frac{1}{7}$

C. $\frac{7}{20}$

D. $\frac{7}{13}$

E. $\frac{13}{20}$

Answer Key

READING

1)

A.   Incorrect. While the author points out that jazz is often associated with New Orleans, he does not indicate that this is a problem or that people should change how they think about jazz.

B.   Correct. The author writes that "[j]azz music was played by and for a more expressive and freed populace than the United States had previously seen." In addition to "the emergence of the flapper," the 1920s saw "the explosion of African American art and culture now known as the Harlem Renaissance."

C.   Incorrect. Though this is mentioned in the passage, it is not the main idea.

D.   Incorrect. Though this is stated at the end of the passage, it is not the main idea.

E.   Incorrect. According to the passage, the first part of this statement is true, but the second part is not: in fact, the Jazz Age "saw major urban centers experiencing new economic, cultural, and artistic vitality" as well as suffrage for American women.

2)

A.   Correct. The author writes that "[j]azz music was played by and for a more expressive and freed populace than the United States had previously seen." In addition to "the emergence of the flapper," the 1920s saw "the explosion of African American art and culture now known as the Harlem Renaissance."

B.   Incorrect. Though these artists are mentioned in the passage, the author does not indicate that they were the most important jazz musicians of the Harlem Renaissance, only that they were important.

C.   Incorrect. Though women's suffrage is mentioned in the passage, the author gives no indication that jazz music was the cause of this change.

D.   Incorrect. Though these artists are mentioned in the passage, the author does not indicate that they supported the movement for women's suffrage.

E.   Incorrect. Though the author says that the Roaring Twenties "saw major urban centers experiencing new economic, cultural, and artistic vitality," he does not identify a causal relationship between jazz music and the country's economic prosperity.

3)

A.   Incorrect. In the first paragraph, the author writes, "In fact, the years between World War I and the Great Depression were known as the Jazz Age, a term coined by F. Scott Fitzgerald in his famous novel *The Great Gatsby*."

B.   Correct. At the end of the first paragraph, the author writes, "Ella Fitzgerald, for example, moved from Virginia to New York City to begin her much-lauded singing career, and jazz pioneer Louis Armstrong got his big break in Chicago."

C.   Incorrect. At the beginning of the second paragraph, the author writes, "Women gained the right to vote and were openly seen drinking and dancing to jazz music. This period marked the emergence of the flapper, a woman determined to make a statement about her new role in society."

D.   Incorrect. Toward the end of the second paragraph, the author writes, "Jazz music also provided the soundtrack for the explosion of African American art and culture now known as the Harlem Renaissance."

E.   Incorrect. In the first sentence, the author writes, "In recent decades, jazz has been associated with New Orleans and festivals like Mardi Gras, but in the 1920s, jazz was a booming trend whose influence reached into many aspects of American culture."

4)

A.   Incorrect. The author writes, "Jazz music also provided the soundtrack for the explosion of African American art and culture now known as the Harlem Renaissance." However, this is not the primary purpose of the passage.

B.   Incorrect. Though the author names many of the important jazz musicians who were playing during the 1920s, this is not the primary purpose of the passage.

C.   Correct. The author opens the passage saying, "In recent decades, jazz has been associated with New Orleans and festivals like Mardi Gras, but in the 1920s, jazz was a booming trend whose influence reached into many aspects of American culture." He then goes on to elaborate on what these movements were.

D.   Incorrect. The author discusses the effects of jazz music on arts and culture in the 1920s but does not go into the history of the art.

E.   Incorrect. The author briefly mentions the modern association of jazz with music festivals like Mardi Gras, but this is not the primary purpose of the passage.

5)

A.   Incorrect. The author states that the term Jazz Age was "coined by F. Scott Fitzgerald in his famous novel *The Great Gatsby*" but does not elaborate on Fitzgerald's relationship to the artists of the age.

B.   Incorrect. The author does not discuss the current popularity of jazz, only that it is often associated with New Orleans.

C.   Correct. The author writes that "[j]azz music was played by and for a more expressive and freed populace than the United States had previously seen." In addition to "the emergence of the flapper," the 1920s saw "the explosion of African American art and culture now known as the Harlem Renaissance."

D.   Incorrect. The passage does not indicate that flappers and African American musicians worked together, only that they both used jazz music as a way to express themselves.

E.   Incorrect. Though the author says that the Roaring Twenties "saw major urban centers experiencing new economic, cultural, and artistic vitality," he does not identify a causal relationship between jazz music and the country's economic prosperity.

6)

A.   Incorrect. The passage implies that "the physical and biological consequences of nuclear war" have impacts that reach much further than the military.

B.   Incorrect. The second part of the second sentence suggests that the consequences of nuclear war—rather than the specific technology of nuclear weapons—are the focus of this student's paper.

C.   Incorrect. The author mentions the decision by world powers to cease testing nuclear weapons in the atmosphere; however, this is only one detail and is likely not the focus of the essay as a whole.

D.   Correct. The passage gives a short history of thermonuclear weapons and then introduces its main topic—the physical and biological consequences of nuclear war.

E.   Incorrect. Though the author mentions a testing ceasefire by world power, this is only one detail of the passage and is likely not the focus of the essay as a whole.

7)

D.   Correct. The word "given" best describes the idea that the gifts have been handed out: "[t]o the lion [Epimetheus] gave strength; to the bird, swiftness; to the fox, sagacity; and so on."

8)

A.   Correct. The author writes, "But people who try to sell you this narrative are wrong. The Civil War was not a battle of cultural identities—it was a battle about slavery."

B.   Incorrect. Though the author describes the cultural differences between the North and South in the first half of the passage, her primary purpose is revealed when she states, "But people who try to sell you this narrative are wrong."

C.   Incorrect. The author makes no comment on the outcome of the Civil War.

D.   Incorrect. The author asserts that, despite the popular identity narrative, the cause of the Civil War was actually very clear: "The Civil War was not a battle of cultural identities—it was a battle about slavery."

E.   Incorrect. The author describes some of the factors that contributed to the Civil War but asserts that only one of those factors was actually the cause of the war: "The Civil War was not a battle of cultural identities—it was a battle about slavery."

9)

B.   Correct. The author states that the South's explanations for the war are "fanciful inventions" designed to cover up history, implying these explanations are imaginative or false.

10)

A.   Incorrect. The author asserts that, despite the popular narrative, cultural differences were not the cause of the Civil War.

B.   **Correct.** The author writes, "The Civil War was not a battle of cultural identities—it was a battle about slavery. All other explanations for the war are either a direct consequence of the South's desire for wealth at the expense of her fellow man or a fanciful invention to cover up this sad portion of our nation's history."

C.   Incorrect. The author does not discuss the strengths of the North or provide any reason for why it won the war.

D.   Incorrect. Though the author mentions these cultural beliefs, she does not suggest that these were the reasons the South was defeated.

E.   Incorrect. Though the author closes with this sentiment, it is not the main idea of the passage.

11)

B.   **Correct.** The author says that the house on Pine Street "had enough space inside but didn't have a big enough yard for [their] three dogs."

12)

A.   **Correct.** The author argues that "every man, woman, and child should learn" to swim, and then explains to the reader why he or she should be able to swim.

13)

B.   **Correct.** In February the service earned $1,100, and in April it earned $200. The difference between the two months is $900.

14)

A.   Incorrect. The author's use of first person and exclamation marks signifies a more personal, less professional tone.

B.   **Correct.** The author uses several markers of casual writing, including the first person, exclamation marks, and informal language.

C.   Incorrect. The author writes that while recent months "have admittedly been a bit slow," she and her team are "hoping for a big summer once school gets out." While she recognizes that business has been slow, she does not seem concerned.

D.   Incorrect. The author takes personal ownership over the business and expresses excitement about the busy Valentine's Day schedule and the upcoming summer.

E.   Incorrect. Though the author mentions that recent months "have admittedly been a bit slow," she remains positive about the summer ahead.

15)

A.   **Correct.** This detail is not stated in the passage.

16)

A.   Incorrect. Thermometers that measure temperature in the ear and temporal artery are mentioned in the passage; however, they are a supporting detail for the author's primary purpose.

B.   **Correct.** In the first paragraph, the author writes, "But what's the best way to get an accurate reading? The answer depends on the situation." She then goes on to describe various options and their applications.

C.   Incorrect. Though this detail is mentioned, it is not the author's primary focus.

D.   Incorrect. The author writes about how many people—not only nurses—use different types of thermometers in different situations.

E.   Incorrect. The author does not go into detail about how to take a baby's temperature.

17)

B.   **Correct.** The author indicates that "[t]he most common way people measure body temperature is orally" but that "[t]here are many situations…when measuring temperature orally isn't an option." She then goes on to describe these situations in the second and third paragraphs.

18)

A.   **Correct.** The final paragraph states that "agitated patients…won't be able to sit still long enough for an accurate reading." The reader can infer that an agitated patient is a patient who is visibly upset, annoyed, or uncomfortable.

B.   Incorrect. While some agitated patients may move quickly, this is not necessarily the meaning of the word in context.

C.   Incorrect. The term "violently ill" does not necessarily explain why a patient would have a difficult time sitting still.

D.   Incorrect. The term "slightly dirty" does not explain why a patient would have a difficult time sitting still.

E.   Incorrect. A patient who was physically comfortable would not have a difficult time sitting still.

19)

A.   **Correct.** The second paragraph of the passage states that "[u]sing the rectum also has the added benefit of providing a much more accurate reading than other locations can provide."

B.   Incorrect. In the final paragraph, the author suggests that "certain people, like agitated patients or fussy babies," might have a difficult time sitting still but does not suggest that this is a problem for "many" people.

C.   Incorrect. In the final paragraph, the author writes that "it's important to check the average temperature for each region, as it can vary by several degrees," but she does not cite this as a reason to use a rectal thermometer.

D.   Incorrect. The author does not mention access to thermometers as a consideration.

E.   Incorrect. The author suggests that "agitated patients" and "fussy babies" who cannot sit still might require that their caretaker use ear or temporal artery thermometers.

20)

D.   **Correct.** The author writes, "the army set high standards: all of the recruits had to be skilled on horseback."

21)

A.   **Correct.** The author states that "[p]opcorn continued to rule the snack food kingdom until the rise in popularity of home televisions during the 1950s" when the industry saw a "decline in sales" as a result of the changing pastimes of the American people.

B.   Incorrect. The author indicates that "the introduction of the mobile popcorn machines" occurred "at the World's Columbian Exposition" after the Great Depression.

C.   Incorrect. The author indicates that the primary reason people consumed popcorn during the Great Depression was that it was advertised as a "wholesome and economical food…a luxury the downtrodden could afford." This implies that the cost, not the luxuriousness, of popcorn was its primary appeal.

D.   Incorrect. The author indicates that "[t]he American love affair with popcorn began in 1912" and only after this did popcorn move "from the theater into fairs and parks."

E.   Incorrect. The author indicates that "[t]he popcorn industry flourished during the Great Depression when it was advertised as a wholesome and economical food" but does not suggest that these are the same reasons popcorn is popular today.

22)

B.   **Correct.** The author states, "For the Aztec Indians who called the caves home, popcorn (or *momochitl*) played an important role in society, both as a food staple and in ceremonies." This implies that the Aztec people popped popcorn both for special occasions ("in ceremonies") and for regular consumption ("as a food staple").

23)

A.   **Correct.** This statement summarizes the entire passage, including the brief history of popcorn in ancient cultures and the growth in the popularity of popcorn in America.

24)

A.   Incorrect. Though the author does discuss the effect of the microwave on the popcorn industry ("it wasn't until microwave popcorn became commercially available in 1981 that at-home popcorn consumption began to grow exponentially"), this is not the primary purpose of the passage.

B.   Incorrect. Though this may be true, it is not the primary purpose of the passage; the author traces the history of popcorn from ancient to modern times.

C.   **Correct.** In the opening paragraph the author writes, "But popcorn isn't just for fun—it's also a multimillion-dollar-a-year industry with a long and fascinating history." The author then goes on to illustrate the history of popcorn from the ancient Aztecs, to early twentieth-century America, to the present day.

D.   Incorrect. Though the author discusses the ancient Aztecs, the rest of the passage is focused on popcorn's history in American culture.

E.   Incorrect. Though the author mentions the rapid growth of the popcorn industry in recent decades ("it wasn't until microwave popcorn became commercially available in 1981 that at-home popcorn consumption began to grow exponentially"), this is not the primary focus of the passage.

25)

A.   Incorrect. The author mentions that popcorn was consumed "both as a food staple and in ceremonies" in Aztec culture but does not tie this to the popcorn industry in the United States.

B.   Incorrect. The author indicates that growth in popularity of home televisions actually hurt the popcorn industry: "Popcorn continued to rule the snack food kingdom until the rise in popularity of home televisions during the 1950s" when the industry saw "a decline in sales."

C.   Correct. The author writes, "The popcorn industry flourished during the Great Depression when it was advertised as a wholesome and economical food."

D.   Incorrect. Though the nutritional value of popcorn is mentioned as a factor in its popularity during the Great Depression, the author does not indicate that this is the reason for its popularity in the United States.

E.   Incorrect. The author indicates that "[t]he popcorn industry reacted to the decline in sales quickly by introducing pre-popped and unpopped popcorn for home consumption" but goes on to say that it was not until three decades later, with the rise in availability of the microwave, that the industry saw significant growth.

26)

A.   Incorrect. The author writes, "In 1948, Herbert Dick and Earle Smith discovered old popcorn dating back 4,000 years in the New Mexico Bat Cave."

B.   Incorrect. The author writes, "The American love affair with popcorn began in 1912, when popcorn was first sold in theaters."

C.   Correct. The author writes, "However, it wasn't until microwave popcorn became commercially available in 1981 that at-home popcorn consumption began to grow exponentially. With the wide availability of microwaves in the United States, popcorn also began popping up in offices and hotel rooms."

D.   Incorrect. The author writes, "However, the home still remains the most popular popcorn eating spot: today, 70 percent of the 16 billion quarts of popcorn consumed annually in the United States are eaten at home."

E.   Incorrect. The author writes, "The popcorn industry flourished during the Great Depression when it was advertised as a wholesome and economical food. Selling for five to ten cents a bag, it was a luxury that the downtrodden could afford."

27)

A.   Incorrect. The passage does not describe the actual artwork at all.

B.   Incorrect. The author names the artist who made the painting but states nothing else about its origin.

C.   Incorrect. While the author does state that there are four versions of the artwork, this is not the primary purpose of the passage.

D. **Correct.** The author writes, "*The Scream of Nature* by Edvard Munch is one of the world's best known and most desirable artworks."

E. Incorrect. The author does name the owners of each version, but this is not the primary purpose of the passage.

---

28)

A. Incorrect. In regional studies, geographers "examine the characteristics of a particular place."

B. Incorrect. In topical studies, geographers "look at a single physical or human feature that impacts the world."

C. Incorrect. In physical studies, geographers "focus on the physical features of Earth."

D. **Correct.** The passage describes human studies as the study of "the relationship between human activity and the environment," which would include farmers interacting with river systems.

E. Incorrect. In physical studies, geographers "focus on the physical features of Earth," not human activity.

---

29)

A. **Correct.** The passage explains what the study of geography involves and outlines its main subdisciplines.

B. Incorrect. The passage does not include a story.

C. Incorrect. The passage does not seek to change readers' opinions or behaviors.

D. Incorrect. The passage provides information and facts but not descriptive details.

E. Incorrect. The passage relies on factual information, not emotional or logical arguments.

---

30)

A. Incorrect. This is only one fact from the passage and does not represent an adequate summary of the passage as a whole.

B. **Correct.** Only this choice summarizes the two main points of the passage: the definition of geography and the breakdown of its subdisciplines.

C. Incorrect. This is only one detail from the passage and does not represent an adequate summary of the passage as a whole.

D. Incorrect. This choice summarizes the second paragraph only and leaves out any summary of the first paragraph.

E. Incorrect. Though this statement is implied by the passage, it does not adequately summarize the passage as a whole.

---

31)

A. **Correct.** The author goes on to describe the shared perspectives of these writers.

B. Incorrect. The author does not indicate the number of writers.

C. Incorrect. The author provides no context that implies they were an organized group, simply that they shared certain traits.

D. Incorrect. The author states that they gathered in one place—Paris.

E.   Incorrect. There is no evidence that this was an educational group.

32)

A.   Incorrect. This answer choice does not fit in the context of the sentence.

B.   Correct. The author writes that "a number of myths about animal pain still plague the field of veterinary medicine and prevent practitioners from making pain management a priority."

C.   Incorrect. The author does not imply that the myths are disturbing, only that they "prevent practitioners from making pain management a priority."

D.   Incorrect. The author indicates that the myths have a negative effect on the treatment of animals, not a positive one.

E.   Incorrect. The author does not imply that the myths are confusing, only that they "prevent practitioners from making pain management a priority."

33)

A.   Incorrect. The author does not seek to make the experience of animals relatable, only to indicate that it is similar to the way humans experience pain and that it should be considered during the course of treatment.

B.   Incorrect. The author does not seek to change the behavior of the reader.

C.   Incorrect. The author does not challenge popular perceptions about the experience of going to the dentist; she only suggests that the experience is similar to that of animals in pain at the veterinarian's office.

D.   Correct. The author writes that "[e]ven the emotional reaction to a painful experience (like being afraid to return to the dentist after an unpleasant visit) is mirrored in animals."

E.   Incorrect. The author does not address the fear that children have of going to the dentist.

34)

A.   Incorrect. The author writes that "pain management is widely accepted as a necessary job of practitioners."

B.   Incorrect. The author does not indicate that veterinarians employ outdated methods of pain management.

C.   Incorrect. The author writes that "pain management is widely accepted as a necessary job of practitioners."

D.   Correct. The author writes, "Although many advancements have been made in research sciences...a number of myths about animal pain still plague the field of veterinary medicine and prevent practitioners from making pain management a priority."

E.   Incorrect. The author does not indicate that veterinarians lack the technology for effective pain management.

35)

A.   Incorrect. The author does not suggest that veterinarians attempt to communicate with animals about their pain.

B.   Correct. The author writes that "veterinarians must be aware of the survival instinct of many animals to mask pain in response to stressful experiences or foreign environments.

For these reasons, diagnostic tools and strategies are instrumental in the effective practice of veterinary medicine."

C.   Incorrect. The author suggests that veterinarians have a responsibility that extends beyond informing pet owners of the importance of close observation.

D.   Incorrect. The author indicates that veterinarians should rely on existing "diagnostic tools and strategies available to today's practitioners" that have been found "to be effective." She does not indicate that veterinarians should invent their own methods for assessing and treating pain.

E.   Incorrect. The author indicates that veterinarians should focus on treating pain in their animal patients.

36)

D.   Correct. The author writes that to diagnose pain in animals, "a veterinarian might make use of an objective pain scale, by which he or she could assess the animal's condition according to a number of criteria. This tool is especially useful throughout the course of treatment, as it provides the practitioner with a quantitative measure for evaluating the effectiveness of various treatment options."

37)

A.   Incorrect. The author of Passage 1 gives no indication that physical damage and pain are unrelated.

B.   Incorrect. The author of Passage 1 does not indicate that presumptive diagnosis is ineffective when used with animals.

C.   Correct. The author of Passage 1 indicates that "according to Grant, the biological mechanisms by which we experience pain are the very same mechanisms by which animals experience pain." This indicates that the author believes that pain and the process of pain management are somewhat similar in animals and humans.

D.   Incorrect. The author of Passage 1 does not indicate that presumptive diagnosis is ineffective when used with animals.

E.   Incorrect. The author of Passage 1 does not indicate that pain diagnosis is more difficult in animals.

38)

A.   Incorrect. The second passage does not reject the claim that pain management should be a priority of veterinarians.

B.   Correct. The author of the first passage writes that "a number of myths about animal pain still plague the field of veterinary medicine and present practitioners from making pain management a priority." This implies that the author believes pain management should be a priority of veterinarians. The second author writes that "diagnostic tools and strategies are instrumental in the effective practice of veterinary medicine" and then goes on to describe some of these tools.

C.   Incorrect. The author of the second passage does not contradict that the myths in the first passage are untrue.

D.   Incorrect. The authors do not discuss shortcomings of veterinary medicine in broad terms; they only address the issue of pain management.

E.   Incorrect. The first author does not discuss early approaches to pain management in animals.

39)

A.   **Correct.** The first author writes, "Grant emphasizes that veterinarians must be aware that a lack of obvious signs does not necessarily suggest that pain is not present: in fact, many animals, especially those that are prey animals in the wild, are likely to conceal their pain out of an instinct to hide weaknesses that may make them easy targets for predators." The second author agrees, saying that "veterinarians must be aware of the survival instinct of many animals to mask pain in response to the foreign environment."

B.   Incorrect. While the first author indicates that pain management should be priority for veterinarians, the second author does not discuss the prioritization of pain management in relation to other responsibilities.

C.   Incorrect. The first author seeks to dispel myths that exist in the world of veterinary medicine; the second author does not.

D.   Incorrect. The second author indicates that thorough examinations must be conducted; the first author does not.

E.   Incorrect. Neither author emphasizes the importance of oral health in animals.

40)

A.   **Correct.** The author writes that animals mask pain in response to the "foreign environment of a veterinary office," implying that the office is unfamiliar to the animal.

41)

A.   **Correct.** Twenty-five students earned an F in science; $(2 \times 25) < 70$.

B.   Incorrect. There are 170 total students with math grades. A majority would be more than half (85). Only 35 students earned a C in math.

C.   Incorrect. Forty students earned a B in reading and 35 students earned a B in math.

D.   Incorrect. The graph does not include information about next year's students.

E.   Incorrect. The same number of students (25) earned C's and D's in science.

42)

A.   Incorrect. The author writes that the protest spread in spite of government attempts to end it.

B.   Incorrect. The author writes, "In Dandi, Gandhi picked up a small chunk of salt and broke British law." Picking up a piece of salt is not itself an extreme act; Gandhi was able to make a big statement with a small action.

C.   **Correct.** The author describes a situation in which civil disobedience had an enormous impact.

D.   Incorrect. The action the author describes occurred in India when it was controlled by Britain, a colonial and nondemocratic power.

E.   Incorrect. The author explains that this event challenged national law and involved tens of thousands of people throughout the country.

43)

B. **Correct.** The paragraph states that "flags are everywhere"; from context, the reader should understand that they are visible at government buildings.

44)

A. Incorrect. The passage notes the importance of vexillology, but this answer leaves out any mention of the FIAV.

B. Incorrect. The passage does not state that the FIAV controls vexillology and flags.

C. **Correct.** The passage discusses the many kinds of flags, and notes that the FIAV was formed to help keep track of the increase in flags with the decolonization movements in the 1960s.

D. Incorrect. The passage mentions flags used by coastal authorities, boaters, and sports fans.

E. Incorrect. The passage does not mention the United Nations at all.

45)

A. **Correct.** It is reasonable to assume that many countries becoming independent around the same time would result in a glut of new flags, and an organization like the FIAV would help keep track of them and avoid problems like duplication of design.

B. Incorrect. There is no reason to assume that flag design was a reason for conflict.

C. Incorrect. The passage does not state that the FIAV ever granted or offered flags to countries, just that it kept track of and studied flags: "There was a need to keep track of new flags." There is no reason to think the FIAV has any authority over countries.

D. Incorrect. There is no reason to assume that nautical flags changed. The passage states, "According to the FIAV, vexillology became an organized field in response to the decolonization and revolutionary movements of the 1960s, when many countries became independent for the first time. There was a need to keep track of new flags, so volunteers stepped up and the organization grew." The context only addresses national flags, not nautical ones.

E. Incorrect. There is nothing to suggest that vexillology became more popular. The passage focuses instead on political and historical movements.

46)

A. Incorrect. While the author states this, it is not the main idea.

B. **Correct.** The author states, "Ignored by the government, an activist group known as Indians of All Tribes sailed to Alcatraz in the early morning hours with eighty-nine men, women, and children." The author goes on to describe the nineteen-month occupation of the island.

C. Incorrect. The author states that up to six hundred people joined the occupation.

D. Incorrect. The author does not describe any violent action toward protestors.

E. Incorrect. While the author does state this, it is not the main idea of the passage.

47)

A. Incorrect. The author does not express an opinion on labor practices.

B.   Incorrect. While the author does explain the advantages of subcontracting for companies, this is not the primary purpose of the passage.

C.   Correct. The author presents the reasons for the debate and both sides of the argument.

D.   Incorrect. The author states that there have been related court cases but does not detail them.

E.   Incorrect. The author does not address any positive benefits of subcontracting for workers.

48)

B.   Correct. The author writes that "[a]s these communities have evolved, the species in them have developed complex, long-term interspecies interactions known as symbiotic relationships." She then goes on to describe the different types of symbiotic relationships that exist.

49)

D.   Correct. The author states that the relationship between remoras and sharks is commensal.

50)

C.   Correct. The author writes, "A relationship where one individual benefits and the other is harmed is known as parasitism."

51)

A.   Correct. The author writes that "[t]here's yet another class of symbiosis that is controversial among scientists" and goes on to say that "many scientists claim the relationships currently described as commensal are just mutualistic or parasitic in ways that haven't been discovered yet." This implies that scientists debate about the topic of commensalism.

B.   Incorrect. The author does not imply that scientists disapprove of or protest commensalism, only that they disagree about whether it truly exists.

C.   Incorrect. The author does not imply that scientists are confused about commensalism, only that they disagree about whether it truly exists.

D.   Incorrect. The author does not imply that scientists are upset about commensalism, only that they disagree about whether it truly exists.

E.   Incorrect. The author does not imply that scientists are offended about commensalism, only that they disagree about whether it truly exists.

52)

A.   Correct. The author writes, "But is it possible for two species to interact and for one to remain completely unaffected? ...In fact, many scientists claim that relationships currently described as commensal are just mutualistic or parasitic in ways that haven't been discovered yet."

B.   Incorrect. The author does not indicate that scientists disagree about the classification of relationships, only that they recognize that they do not fully understand all relationships yet and may, therefore, be classifying some of them based on incomplete information.

C.   Incorrect. The author does not indicate that the example of remoras and sharks is the reason for the controversy about commensalism, only that it illustrates this controversy well.

D.   Incorrect. The author does indicate that the controversy around commensalism is limited to discussions of animal species only.

E.   Incorrect. The author writes that commensalism is controversial because scientists are not sure if it is "possible for two species to interact and for one to remain completely unaffected"; however, this does not imply that scientists think animals are altogether incapable of interspecies interaction.

53)

D.   Correct. The author writes, "The bacteria, fungi, insects, plants, and animals that live together in a habitat have evolved to share a pool of limited resources...As these communities have evolved, the species in them have developed complex, long-term interspecies interactions known as symbiotic relationships."

54)

A.   Incorrect. There is no evidence that the protest movement was successful; in fact, the passage implies the opposite.

B.   Incorrect. While the author states that Western countries observed the events in China, there is no evidence they became involved.

C.   Incorrect. There is no evidence in the passage that factory workers had any involvement beyond "cheering on" the protestors.

D.   Incorrect. There is no evidence the government objected to the military's actions.

E.   Correct. The author writes, "it seemed to be the beginning of a political revolution in China, so the world was stunned when, on July 4, Chinese troops and security police stormed the square," stifling any possibility of democratic revolution.

55)

A.   Correct. The passage describes how the closing of the border affected the geography of the city and the lives of Berliners.

B.   Incorrect. The author does not explain why the border was closed.

C.   Incorrect. The author does not describe the response to the border closing.

D.   Incorrect. The author explains that the East German army closed off West Berlin using barbed wire and fences, but this is not the primary purpose of the passage.

E.   Incorrect. While the author does explain how the border was closed, there is no further discussion of its history.

56)

B.   Correct. The final sentence of the passage is an opinion; others might argue that there are more troubling periods in Germany's history. The other statements are all facts from the passage.

WRITING

USAGE

1)

C. **Correct.** *Plays* is a singular verb and does not correctly pair with the plural subject *men*; *men dress* and *play*.

2)

B. **Correct.** *African* is derived from the name of a place (Africa) and is therefore a proper noun that needs to be capitalized.

3)

E. **Correct.** No errors are present in this sentence.

4)

C. **Correct.** The preposition *over* does not accurately illustrate the relationship between the vaccine and the young boy's infection; more appropriate would be the preposition *by*.

5)

B. **Correct.** The verb in this sentence (*is*) must be edited in order to create agreement between the subject (*items*) and the verb (which should be *are*).

6)

B. **Correct.** The subject of this sentence is the singular *breed*; though it is separated from the subject by an adjectival phrase, the verb must also be singular (*has*).

7)

D. **Correct.** Because it is a negative, *no other* inaccurately discounts the first negative (*not*) and creates a double negative (*could not afford no other*); it should be changed to *any other*.

8)

E. **Correct.** No error exists in this sentence.

9)

A. **Correct.** A comma should not be included in this location, as it separates the subject (*photographer*) and the verb (*specializes*).

10)

B. **Correct.** *Countries'* is a plural possessive but should be acting as a plural subject; the correct format of the word is *countries* (*around the world*).

11)

B.   **Correct.** *Continued* is a past-tense verb; however, it should be present tense (*continues*) in order to align with the time mentioned later in the sentence (*even today*).

12)

D.   **Correct.** Because the people *of many countries* are benefiting, multiple populations are benefiting: *the population[s] of many countries*.

Sentence Correction

13)

A.   **Correct.** *In addition* is the appropriate introductory phrase to signify the additive relationship between the two clauses.

14)

C.   **Correct.** In this choice, all items in the list are nouns (*dearth*, *lack*, and *list*), followed by prepositions (*of*) and objects of the prepositions (*wins*, *time*, and *clients*).

15)

E.   **Correct.** *Invented*, the past participle of *invent*, appropriately introduces this participial phrase that provides more information about the subject of the sentence (*stethoscope*).

16)

B.   **Correct.** *Which* is used correctly here to introduce an additional, nonrestrictive clause about an element of the sentence (the musical).

17)

A.   **Correct.** *Is* is a present-tense verb, used correctly to refer to current mindsets; *than* is used correctly to show comparison.

18)

E.   **Correct.** *Commonly* is an adverb describing *confused*, which is an adjective describing *painters*.

19)

B.   **Correct.** The three phrases share a structure; they are parallel adjectives.

20)

D.   **Correct.** The three phrases have a similar (parallel) structure (verb + direct object).

21)

E.   **Correct.** Because the sentence states a general fact, it should be written in present tense (*hot chocolate is made*).

22)

E.   **Correct.** The semicolon is used appropriately here to join two independent, related clauses; *in fact* signifies an interesting detail to follow.

23)

C.   **Correct.** Because the sentence states a general fact (how seat belts work), it should be written in present tense.

24)

A.   **Correct.** *Ranking* sets off a participial phrase that provides additional information about the subject of the sentence (*Prince*).

REVISION IN CONTEXT

25)

A.   **Correct.** This information is unnecessary and detracts from the point of the passage.

26)

C.   **Correct.** This is the clearest, most concise choice for communicating this idea.

27)

A.   Incorrect. *Therefore* does not fit in the context of this sentence, as no cause-and-effect relationship exists.

B.   **Correct.** *In fact* can be used correctly in this instance to draw attention to interesting information that builds on the previous sentence.

C.   Incorrect. *However* does not fit in the context of this sentence, as no contradictory relationship exists.

D.   Incorrect. *In addition* does not fit in the context of this sentence, as this sentence builds on the previous one and does not introduce a new idea.

E.   Incorrect. *Consequently* does not fit in the context of this sentence, as no cause-and-effect relationship exists.

28)

A.   Incorrect. The sentence provides important information about two scientists who point to science fiction as the inspiration for their work.

B.   Incorrect. *Always* is unnecessary to the reader's understanding of the sentence.

C.   **Correct.** *His* should become *their* because the work belongs to two people (Goddard and Szilard).

D.   Incorrect. The phrase inside the dashes is not grammatically necessary, but it is helpful to the reader's understanding of the sentence.

E.   Incorrect. *Futuristic* is an adjective, used correctly here to modify *novels*.

29)

A.   Incorrect. This choice is too specific, as only one sentence of the final paragraph relates to transportation.

B.   Incorrect. This sentence adds very little to the meaning of the paragraph.

C.   Incorrect. The tone of this sentence is conversational, and it does not fit with the rest of the passage.

D.   Correct. This choice provides a brief but interesting overview of the information to come.

E.   Incorrect. This sentence is not relevant, as all of the inventions being discussed were, in the end, realistic.

30)

A.   Correct. This sentence relates directly to the overall idea of the passage—that science fiction has a natural influence on real life.

B.   Incorrect. This sentence does not relate to the overall topic of the passage—the relationship between science fiction and reality.

C.   Incorrect. Though this may be true, the sentence does not provide any useful information and detracts from the main idea of the passage.

D.   Incorrect. This sentence is inappropriately argumentative when compared with the rest of the passage, and it detracts from the main idea of the passage.

E.   Incorrect. This sentence is too general and provides no additional insight to the reader.

31)

A.   Correct. As it is written, *More recently* provides the reader with information about the time period being referred to as well as its relationship to the time period that was discussed in the previous sentence.

B.   Incorrect. *These days* in a colloquial expression used to refer to the present day; it does not agree with the meaning the author hopes to convey.

C.   Incorrect. *Therefore* incorrectly suggests a cause-and-effect relationship between this sentence and the preceding sentence.

D.   Incorrect. *On the other hand* incorrectly suggests a contradictory relationship between this sentence and the preceding sentence.

E.   Incorrect. *In addition* incorrectly suggests an additive relationship between this sentence and the preceding sentence.

32)

A.   Incorrect. The final phrase *the changeling* is incorrectly set off from its descriptor with only a comma.

B.   Correct. The final phrase *the changeling* is appropriately set off from the rest of the sentence—its descriptor—with a colon.

C.   Incorrect. The dashes in this sentence incorrectly set off information that is essential to the meaning.

D.   Incorrect. This choice creates a fragment by placing *the changeling* in its own sentence.

E.   Incorrect. This choice includes an unnecessary comma after blame, which separates the essential adverbial phrase (*when individuals begin...*) from the rest of the sentence.

33)

C.   **Correct.** This choice incorrectly joins two independent clauses with a comma (*changelings were...* and *they were left...*).

34)

A.   Incorrect. The sentence provides a meaningful conclusion to the paragraph by explaining why people may have been invested in the changeling legend.

B.   **Correct.** *Explanation* adds an important detail about what the demonstrative pronoun *this* refers to.

C.   Incorrect. *Families* is used correctly in the sentence to signify multiple families and does not need to be changed.

D.   Incorrect. *Whose* is used correctly in the sentence to signify possession (the children *of* the families) and does not need to be changed.

E.   Incorrect. *Ailments* and *illnesses* are synonyms, so no change is necessary.

35)

A.   **Correct.** As written, the sentence acts appropriately as an introductory sentence, providing a summary of the topic that will be discussed; additionally, it gives meaning to the phrase *for example* in sentence 9.

36)

A.   Incorrect. This choice creates a comma splice by combining two independent clauses with a comma.

B.   Incorrect. This choice combines the independent clauses correctly with a comma and a conjunction; however, the meaning of the conjunction *so* suggests a cause-and-effect relationship, which does not exist here.

C.   Incorrect. This choice combines the independent clauses correctly with a comma and a conjunction; however, the meaning of the conjunction *but* suggests a contradictory relationship, which does not exist here.

D.   Incorrect. This choice combines the independent clauses correctly with a semicolon and an introductory word; however, the meaning of *however* suggests a contradictory relationship, which does not exist here.

E.   **Correct.** The choice correctly joins the independent clauses with a colon, signifying that the information in the second clause somehow builds or expands on the first.

Research Skills

A. **Correct.** APA Style is derived from guidelines published by the American Psychological Association; it should be used when writing in a field of the social sciences.

B. Incorrect. MLA Style is derived from guidelines published by the Modern Language Association; it should be used when writing in the fields of liberal arts or humanities.

C. Incorrect. Though Chicago Style can be used for many types of papers, it is most commonly seen in the fields of history and anthropology and is not common for psychology research.

D. Incorrect. Students should receive explicit instruction in the various style guides and should be instructed on the appropriate use of each.

E. Incorrect. Style guides should be used in order to provide information on how students should cite their research.

38

A. Incorrect. A paper that reviews other studies is not introducing unique or novel information and is considered a secondary source.

B. Incorrect. Because the journalist is interpreting the events and interviews to draw conclusions about the government's efforts, the article would be considered a secondary source.

C. Incorrect. Because the review critiques another author's work, it would be considered a secondary source.

D. **Correct.** Because the results of the study are original and are being published by the author of the study, this paper would be considered a primary source.

E. Incorrect. A summary of another's work is considered a secondary source.

39

A. **Correct.** Because the art historian must filter the information (the art) through his or her own perspective, this interpretive essay would be considered a secondary source.

B. Incorrect. Because court transcripts come directly from the proceedings in the courtroom (without interpretation), they would be considered primary source documents.

C. Incorrect. Because the journal entries reflect the student's personal experience of the event, they would be considered primary sources.

D. Incorrect. Because the video provides a firsthand account of the aftermath, it would be considered a primary source.

E. Incorrect. Because the audio recording provides a firsthand account of the politician's admission (without interpretation), it would be considered a primary source.

40

A. Incorrect. Population variance is relevant to the topic of bird migration.

B. Incorrect. A discussion of different types of migration is relevant to the reader's understanding of bird migration.

C. Incorrect. Methods of movement are relevant to the topic of bird migration.

D. **Correct.** Though it is interesting, the history of humanity's understanding of bird migration is not necessarily relevant to an essay about bird migration.

E. Incorrect. Variations in migration patterns are relevant to an essay about bird migration.

ARGUMENTATIVE ESSAY

History provides countless examples of crowds that have become unruly, dangerous, even deadly. However, a commanding leader can make a difference. When a charismatic leader harnesses the emotions of the crowd, he or she can stir it up or calm it down with thoughtful and evocative words and actions. During the Great Depression, US President Franklin D. Roosevelt's speeches and "Fireside Chats" calmed Americans fearful of losing their savings and quelled financial panic. However, powerful speakers have the power to trigger violence. In the 1930s, Adolf Hitler's nationalist speeches in Germany inspired anti-Semitism, racism, and violent acts like Kristallnacht. A large crowd can remain calm in an emotional situation, but only with the right leadership.

Consumer panic makes an economic crisis into a catastrophe when people withdraw their funds from banks all at once, and social unrest can soon follow. FDR's public speeches and radio addresses, known as "Fireside Chats," were intended to calm the public while allowing bank reform and economic recovery to occur. Famously, in describing emergency measures to close the banks, he explained economic policy in plain language, reassuring Americans that their money would still be available when banks reopened. He also stayed positive and optimistic, using euphemisms like "bank holiday" and "inconvenience." His word choice and demeanor encouraged people to stay calm and cooperate with financial reforms. In fact, in his inaugural address, he proclaimed that there was "nothing to fear but fear itself," inspiring faith rather than panic in a time of national crisis when social unrest was feared.

On the other hand, Adolf Hitler rose to power in Germany on a platform of nationalism and discrimination. At the time, much like the United States, Germany was suffering from an economic depression and struggling to rebuild following the First World War. Unlike FDR, Hitler used negative language and scapegoated minority groups, especially Jewish people. He encouraged violence among his followers such as book burnings, property damage, and deadly acts against Jewish people and other minority groups. As the Nazis became more powerful, Jewish people were subject to discriminatory laws and oppressive treatment. Jewish businesses were attacked and looted on Kristallnacht. Hitler's harsh rhetoric had contributed to a social and political environment where this abuse was acceptable, and it led to the Holocaust.

Overall, crowds are driven by emotion, and even people who remain rational within them cannot take control. Some people helped the Jews and other persecuted people in Nazi Germany, but they did so in secret, no match for the power of Hitler and Nazi ideology over the nation. Yet, as shown by FDR's leadership during the Great Depression, it is possible for a huge group—an entire nation—to stave off irrational, panicky behavior even with something as important as money. A crowd, despite its essential emotional nature, can be rendered rational and calm by the right leader.

SOURCE-BASED ESSAY

As public bicycle share programs (PBSPs) increase in popularity, significant debate has emerged over helmet requirements in cities that implement these systems. Both sides of the debate agree that helmets improve safety for bicycle riders. Historically, mandatory bicycle laws have greatly increased helmet usage and had a significant impact on reducing traumatic brain injuries. Both sides of the debate also agree that PBSPs provide both transportation and environmental benefits to cities. They can decrease congestion and provide low-cost and flexible transportation options for commuters and tourists. Finally, both perspectives agree that mandatory helmet laws hamper the development of bicycle-based urban public transportation, by discouraging riders from partaking in the system. The conflict between the two camps centers on how cities should balance their responsibility to individual safety and public policy goals.

Cities with mandatory helmet laws have struggled to get their programs off the ground, experiencing significantly decreased participation rates. For example, according to Passage 1, Melbourne, which has a mandatory helmet law, has a participation rate anywhere from 67 to 83 percent lower than London, which has no such law. Without extensive participation, the societal benefits of PBSPs are greatly diminished. While Melbourne's system still offers a transportation alternative, it is clearly not viewed as a viable one by most of the population, and so provides little benefit in that way. Also, with such markedly low participation rates, impact on congestion and pollution would be negligible.

On the other hand, PBSP riders typically do not have extensive experience riding in urban environments whose increased traffic can pose greater risk of an accident. According to Passage 2, a recent study shows that PBSPs that do not mandate helmets increase the chance of a rider suffering a traumatic brain injury during a biking accident. This increase could potentially create new policy problems as it impacts one of the city government's primary goals: ensuring the safety of its people.

Some cities have attempted to make helmets more accessible by installing helmet vending machines near bike stations or even leaving free helmets out for riders, according to Passage 1. However, according to Passage 2, few people take advantage of these options. This indicates that people would rather opt out than use a helmet; perhaps issues beyond accessibility factor into the equation. For example, while people are willing to share bicycles, they may not be willing to share headgear, which could be perceived as unsanitary. Or riders could be concerned with fitting, as helmets come in a variety of sizes. The nature of PBSPs can also be a factor. The majority of PBSP users are casual riders according to Passage 1, who are attracted by the flexibility and ease of use the programs. This includes tourists or commuters who perhaps did not even intend to ride a bike when they set out. Even if it does not actually require any increased effort, such users may simply feel that helmet laws detract from the open nature of PBSPs.

Because both sides of the debate agree that helmet usage is preferable and that PBSPs are beneficial, several questions on this topic are open to further research. For example, researchers should examine the overall number of injuries in cities with PBSPs compared to those without, and how the volume of users impacts both rider and vehicle safety on the road. They could also look at how the modification of roads to accommodate bikers by installing protected bike lanes, for example, impacts safety numbers. Finally, researchers could explore alternative ways to encourage helmet use beyond legislation.

MATHEMATICS

1)

B. **Correct.** The prime factorization of 45 is $3 \times 3 \times 5$ and the prime factorization of 22 is 2×11. The two numbers have no prime factors in common. Because 1 is a factor of every number, their greatest common factor is 1.

2)

C. **Correct.** Use the formula for percent change.

$$\text{percent change} = \frac{\text{amount of change}}{\text{original amount}}$$

$$= \frac{7375 - 7250}{7250} = 0.017 = \textbf{1.7\%}$$

3)

A. **Correct.** Adding a zero at the end of a number after a decimal does not change the number's value.

D. **Correct.** The decimal part ends in the hundredths place, so it is correct to place the decimal over 100.

4)

C. **Correct.** Write out each number to find the largest.

A. 9299 ones = 9299

B. 903 tens = 9030

C. **93 hundreds = 9300**

D. 9 thousands = 9000

E. 9 thousandths = 0.009

5)

D. **Correct.** Set up a proportion and solve.

$$\frac{8}{650} = \frac{12}{x}$$

$$8x = (650)(12)$$

$$x = \textbf{975 miles}$$

6)

B. **Correct.** The slope 0.0293 gives the increase in passenger car miles (in billions) for each year that passes. Multiply this value by 5 to find the increase that occurs over 5 years: $5(0.0293) = \textbf{0.1465 billion miles}$.

7)

E. **Correct.** Use the graph to find the number of months Chicago had less than 3 inches of rain year, and then find the average.

Months with < 3 inches of rain in Chicago: {7, 8, 10, 7, 9, 10, 10}

$$\frac{7 + 8 + 10 + 7 + 9 + 10 + 10}{7} = 8.7 \approx \textbf{9}$$

8)

B. **Correct.** Calculate the volume of water in tank A.

$$V = l \times w \times h$$

$$5 \times 10 \times 1 = 50 \text{ ft}^3$$

Find the height this volume would reach in tank B.

$$V = l \times w \times h$$

$$50 = 5 \times 5 \times h$$

$$\textbf{\textit{h} = 2 ft}$$

9)

A. **Correct.** Find the 5th term.

$$-27 - 9 = -36$$

$$-36 \times -3 = 108$$

Find the 6th term.

$$108 - (-27) = 135$$

$$135 \times -3 = \textbf{-405}$$

10)

$$1\frac{3}{8}$$

Subtract the amount she used from the number of yards she started with.

$$6 - 4\tfrac{5}{8} = 5\tfrac{8}{8} - 4\tfrac{5}{8} = \mathbf{1\tfrac{3}{8} \ yd}$$

11)

E. **Correct.** The statement $17 + 15 = 32$ is an example of two odd numbers that give a positive number when added.

12)

D. **Correct.** Find the area of the complete rectangle and subtract the area of the missing corners.

rectangle: $A = lw = (20 + 2 + 2) \times (10 + 2 + 2) = 336$ cm²

corners: $A = 4(lw) = 4(2 \times 2) = 16$ cm²

$336 - 16 = \mathbf{320 \ cm^2}$

13)

A, C, and E are correct. $4 + 10x = 10x + 4$ by the commutative property.

$2(5x + 2) = 10x + 4$ by the distributive property.

$6x + 7 + 4x - 3 = 10x + 4$ by combining like terms.

14)

A. **Correct.** If the ratio of nurses to doctors is 3:1, then the total number of nurses and doctors must be a multiple of 4 (as $3 + 1 = 4$).

15)

B. **Correct.** Using the cars with the largest capacity first, add together the seats in the cars until there are 20.

$6 + 5 = 11$

$6 + 5 + 5 = 16$

$6 + 5 + 5 + 5 = 21$

The fewest number of cars that will seat 20 people is **4 cars**.

16)

A. **Correct.**

$$3(2y + 1) + 3 = 4(y - 2)$$
$$6y + 3 + 3 = 4y - 8$$
$$6y + 6 = 4y - 8$$
$$6y = 4y - 14$$
$$2y = -14$$
$$\mathbf{y = -7}$$

17)

C. **Correct.** Subtract to find the number of questions the student answered incorrectly.

$150 - 129 = 21$

Use the formula for percentages.

$\text{percent} = \dfrac{\text{part}}{\text{whole}} = \dfrac{21}{150} = 0.14 = \mathbf{14\%}$

18)

A. **Correct.**

$$6x - 7 = 5(2x + 1)$$
$$6x - 7 = 10x + 5$$
$$6x = 10x + 12$$
$$-4x = 12$$
$$\mathbf{x = -3}$$

19)

C. **Correct.** Plug the given values into the equation and solve for t.

$$d = v \times t$$
$$4000 = 500 \times t$$
$$\mathbf{t = 8 \ hours}$$

20)

B. **Correct.** Add the area of the semicircle and the area of the triangle.

semicircle: $A = \dfrac{\pi r^2}{2} = \dfrac{\pi(3)^2}{2} = 4.5\pi$

triangle: $A = \dfrac{1}{2}bh = \dfrac{1}{2}(6)(10) = 30$

total area = $\mathbf{30 + 4.5\pi}$

21)

A. **Correct.** Justin's profit will be his income minus his expenses. He will earn $40 for each lawn, or $40m$. He pays $35 in expenses each week, or 35*x*.

profit = **40*m* − 35*x***

22)

D. **Correct.** Solve the problem using a proportion. The ratio of diet to regular is 1:3, so the total number of sodas is a multiple of 4.

$\frac{3}{4} = \frac{x}{24}$

$4x = 3(24)$

$4x = 72$

$x = 18$

23)

B. **Correct.** Multiply the cost per pound by the number of pounds purchased to find the cost of each fruit.

apples: 2(1.89) = 3.78

oranges: 1.5(2.19) = 3.285

3.78 + 3.285 = 7.065 = **$7.07**

24)

D. **Correct.** The given sequence is formed by subtracting 3 from the previous value in the sequence.

25)

222.5

Multiply the car's speed by the time traveled to find the distance.

1.5(65) = 97.5 miles

2.5(50) = 125 miles

97.5 + 125 = **222.5 miles**

26)

B. **Correct.** Multiply each side by 2.

$4x = 3$

$2(4x) = 2(3)$

$8x = 6$

27)

C. **Correct.** Find the measure of each angle.

m∠*w* = 180 − (70 + 40) = 70°

m∠*x* = 70°

m∠*y* = 180 − 40 = 140°

m∠*z* = 40°

∠*w* ≅ ∠*x*

28)

C. **Correct.** The *y*-intercept (where the line crosses the *y*-axis) will have an *x* value of 0. This eliminates choices A, B, and D.

Plug *x* = 0 into the equation, and solve for *y* to find the *y*-intercept:

$7y - 42(0) + 7 = 0$

$7y = -7$

$y = -1$

The *y*-intercept is (0, −1).

29)

$\frac{3}{4}$

Add the fractions and subtract the result from the amount of flour Allison started with.

$2\frac{1}{2} + \frac{3}{4} = \frac{5}{2} + \frac{3}{4} = \frac{10}{4} + \frac{3}{4} = \frac{13}{4}$

$4 - \frac{13}{4} = \frac{16}{4} - \frac{13}{4} = \frac{3}{4}$ **cups**

30)

B. **Correct.** Find a common denominator and subtract.

$\frac{4}{5} - \frac{1}{3} = \frac{4}{5}\left(\frac{3}{3}\right) - \frac{1}{3}\left(\frac{5}{5}\right) = \frac{12}{15} - \frac{5}{15}$

$= \frac{7}{15}$

31)

B. **Correct.** The sides in equilateral triangles are all the same length, and the sides of a square are all the same length. Because the triangles and the square share a side, all the lines in the figure are the same length. The perimeter can be used to find the length of one side:

60 inches ÷ 6 = 10 inches

Multiply two sides of the square to find its area:

10 in × 10 in = **100 in²**

32)

E. **Correct.** All the points lie on the circle, so each line segment is a radius. The sum of the 4 lines will be 4 times the radius.

$r = \frac{75}{2} = 37.5$

$4r = \textbf{150}$

33)

B. **Correct.** Find the area of all sides of the shed. Two walls measure 5 feet by 7 feet; the other two walls measure 4 feet by 7 feet.

$A = 2l_1w_1 + 2l_2w_2$

$A = 2(5 \text{ ft})(7 \text{ ft}) + 2(4 \text{ ft})(7 \text{ ft})$

$A = 70 \text{ ft}^2 + 56 \text{ ft}^2 = \textbf{126 ft}^2$

34)

D. **Correct.** Use the volume to find the length of the cube's side.

$V = s^3$

$343 = s^3$

$s = 7 \text{ m}$

Find the area of each side.

$7(7) = 49 \text{ m}^2$

Multiply the area of each side by 6 to find the total surface area.

$49(6) = \textbf{294 m}^2$

35)

B. **Correct.** Find the sum of the 13 numbers whose mean is 30.

$13 \times 30 = 390$

Find the sum of the 8 numbers whose mean is 42.

$8 \times 42 = 336$

Find the sum and mean of the remaining 5 numbers.

$390 - 336 = 54$

$\frac{54}{5} = \textbf{10.8}$

36)

A. **Correct.** Subtract the amount of the bills from the amount in the checking account.

$792.00 + 84.63 + 112.15 = 988.78$

$2386.52 - 988.78 = \textbf{\$1397.74}$

37)

C. **Correct.** Use the formula for percent change.

$\text{percent change} = \frac{\text{amount of change}}{\text{original amount}}$

$= \frac{680 - 425}{425} = 0.6 = \textbf{60\%}$

38)

D. **Correct.** Set up a proportion and solve.

$\frac{1}{280} = \frac{1.5}{x}$

$x = (280)(1.5)$

$x = \textbf{420}$

39)

A. **Correct.** Dividing by 100 produces the same result as multiplying by $\frac{1}{100}$.

$n \div 100 = \frac{n}{100}$

$n \times \frac{1}{100} = \frac{n}{100}$

40)

A. **Correct.** Plug in the given value for y and solve for x.

$5x + 2 = 2y$

$5x + 2 = 2(6)$

$5x + 2 = 12$

$5x + 2 - 2 = 12 - 2$

$5x = 10$

$\frac{5x}{5} = \frac{10}{5}$

$x = \textbf{2}$

41)

B and E are correct. Combine like terms.

$3n + 2n = 5n$

$n + n + n + n + n = 5n$

42)

A, C, and E are correct. 790 is divisible by 2 because it is an even number. It is divisible by both 5 and 10 because the digit in the ones place is 0.

43)

E. **Correct.** Divide and find the digit in the hundredths place.

$21.563 \div 8 = \mathbf{2.695375}$

44)

0.65

To find the average, add the rainfall amounts and divide by 5.

$\frac{0.75 + 1.25 + 0 + 0.5 + 0.75}{5} = \mathbf{0.65}$

45)

B. **Correct.** Convert each fraction in the problem to a decimal.

$5\frac{1}{4} = 5.25$

$5\frac{1}{2} = 5.5$

Convert each answer choice to a decimal, and find the value between 5.25 and 5.5.

Choice A: $5\frac{5}{8} = 5.625$

Choice B: $5\frac{7}{20} = \mathbf{5.35}$

Choice C: $5\frac{3}{4} = 5.75$

Choice D: $5\frac{1}{10} = 5.1$

Choice E: $5\frac{8}{15} = 5.533$

46)

D. **Correct.** List all the even integers greater than 10 and less than 25 in

ascending order. The median is the value in the middle.

12, 14, 16, **18**, 20, 22, 24

47)

B. **Correct.** The answer choices are in liters, so convert gallons to liters.

$2 \text{ gal} \times \frac{3.785 \text{ L}}{1 \text{ gal}} = 7.57 \text{ L}$

Subtract to find the difference in liters.

$10 \text{ L} - 7.57 \text{ L} = \mathbf{2.43 \text{ L}}$

48)

A. **Correct.** Use dimensional analysis to convert feet to miles and seconds to hours.

$\frac{15 \text{ ft}}{\text{sec}} \times \frac{3600 \text{ sec}}{1 \text{ hr}} \times \frac{1 \text{ mi}}{5280 \text{ ft}}$

$\approx \mathbf{10.2 \text{ mph}}$

49)

C. **Correct.** The diagonals of a rectangle create two sets of congruent triangles.

50)

B. **Correct.** Find all the numbers in the shaded region by identifying the factors of 24 and 28.

24: 1, 2, 3, 4, 6, 8, 12, 24

28: 1, 2, 4, 7, 14, 28

The set of numbers in the shaded region is {1, 2, 4}, so the total number of possible outcomes is 3.

Use the formula for probability.

P(selecting 2)

$= \frac{\text{number of favorable outcomes}}{\text{total number of possible outcomes}}$

$= \frac{1}{3}$

51)

6

In algebraic terms, the ratio can be expressed with the following equation:

$9x + 2x + 1x = 36$

Here, x represents some common factor by which each number of employees was divided to reduce the ratio. Solve for x.

$9x + 2x + 1x = 36$

$12x = 36$

$x = 3$

The number of hosts equals $2x$.

$2x = 2(3) = 6$

52)

C. **Correct.** Use the area to find the length of one side of the square.

$A = s^2$

$5,625 = s^2$

$\sqrt{5,625} = s$

$s = 75$ ft

Now multiply the side length by 4 to find the perimeter.

$P = 4s$

$P = 4(75 \text{ ft.}) = \textbf{300 ft}$

53)

D. **Correct.** The formula for the circumference of a circle is $C = 2\pi r$.

Because $d = 2r$, this formula can be rewritten:

$C = \pi d$

$50 \text{ ft} = \pi d$

$d = \frac{50}{\pi}$

54)

8

Use the equation for the perimeter of a rectangle.

$P = 2l + 2w$

$42 = 2(13) + 2w$

$\textbf{w = 8}$

55)

A. **Correct.** Find the amount the state will spend on infrastructure and education, and then find the difference.

infrastructure $= 0.2(3,000,000,000) = 600,000,000$

education $= 0.18(3,000,000,000) = 540,000,000$

$600,000,000 - 540,000,000 = \textbf{\$60,000,000}$

56)

C. **Correct.** Use the equation for probability.

P(an event)

$= \frac{\text{number of favorable outcomes}}{\text{total number of possible outcomes}}$

$P = \frac{7}{5 + 7 + 8} = \frac{7}{20}$

For your second Praxis Core Skills practice test, follow the link below: http://www.cirrustestprep.com/praxis-core-academic-skills-for-educators-online-resources.